Choosing to Heal

Choosing to Heal

Using Reality Therapy in the Treatment
of Sexually Abused Children

Laura Ellsworth

Routledge
Taylor & Francis Group
New York   London

Routledge
Taylor & Francis Group
270 Madison Avenue
New York, NY 10016

Routledge
Taylor & Francis Group
2 Park Square
Milton Park, Abingdon
Oxon OX14 4RN

Printed in the United States of America on acid-free paper
10 9 8 7 6 5 4 3 2 1

International Standard Book Number-10: 0-415-95614-5 (Softcover)
International Standard Book Number-13: 978-0-415-95614-7 (Softcover)

Visit the Taylor & Francis Web site at
http://www.taylorandfrancis.com

and the Routledge Web site at
http://www.routledge.com

To Jake and Jade,
the two best choices I ever made.
Love,
Mommy

Contents

Foreword

We seem more and more to be living in a "Well, it all depends" kind of world. This attitude hasn't developed necessarily by edict or legal action, but is more likely to result from inaction on the part of people who rarely want to take a firm stand on important issues. For example, the vast majority of people usually decry the unbearable inhumanity of murder. When one person willingly takes the life of one or more people, most of us willingly agree to the imprisonment or even to taking the life of the convicted murderer. However, in the best "Well, it all depends" world we can imagine, during wartime many of these same good folks cheer the killer or killers, and take great pride in applauding their efforts. The nation's highest medal is often awarded to the most successful takers of life, because it all depends on the circumstances. One of the strongest defenses in a murder trial is when the defendant can prove that the killing was justified on the grounds of self-defense.

Another popular "Well, it all depends" example is the taking of someone else's property. In one circumstance, this action is referred to as stealing and is punishable by a fine or even imprisonment. In another circumstance, it is found to be legally acceptable and recognized as "the right of public domain," a kind of "What's mine is mine and what's yours is mine if I can prove that I will use it for the good of a greater group."

On the other side of this kind of thinking is a situation on which there is nearly total agreement, the universally despised sexual abuse of and assault on children. It is considered wrong in this society and all others. It is so generally accepted as wrong that even the most despicable of institutionalized criminals see it as unacceptable and will attack the perpetrators.

Laura Ellsworth has provided a new and valuable resource for helping sexually abused children. Her 16 years of experience in the field of counseling, especially in the treatment of sexually abused children and their abusers, represents a tremendous amount of real, tested, and successful techniques that will be of enormous assistance to counselors who work in this field.

J. Robert Cockrum, Ed.D.

Acknowledgments

It is difficult to know where to start in thanking everyone who contributed to the book and motivated me to write it. It really began in my own childhood with the people who molded and helped me to be a survivor, therapist, and writer.

- Ada Gray: My grandmother, now gone but never forgotten, who showed me that women can be strong, resilient, and loving.
- Bob and Jane Cockrum: You both introduced me to reality therapy and continue to teach and inspire me in so many ways. Bob, your time and effort put into editing helped make this a quality book.
- Bob Hoglund: Your meticulous attention to detail and editing of this book was critical to making me look like a "real writer."
- Kay Nix, a.k.a. Mom: Your typing skills, ability to decipher my handwriting, worksheet development, and caretaking of the two most wonderful children in the world made this process quicker and less stressful.
- Bob Wubbolding, Jon Erwin, Bob Sullo, and Nancy Buck inspired me through your own writings to add to the Reality Therapy/Choice Theory library.
- David G. Voyles and David R. Voyles, my daddy and brother, whom I adore, have shown me that men who love and honor their daughters can help them produce great things.
- George Zimmar: My wonderful editor, for seeing the value in this book and giving a new writer a chance.

About the Author

Laura Ellsworth has specialized in the treatment of child sexual abuse for over 16 years. She has helped children, their families, and adult survivors of childhood sexual abuse cope through individual, group, family and education modalities of treatment. She provides training for therapists, foster parents, schools and community organizations in how to effectively deal with children who have been sexually abused. Laura graduated from Kentucky Wesleyan College with a bachelor's degree in psychology. She earned her master's degree in psychology from the University of Kentucky. Laura resides in Evansville, Indiana. She may be contacted through her website www.choosingtoheal.com.

Introduction

The treatment of sexually abused children often poses a dilemma for mental health professionals. Limited resources and inadequate training opportunities routinely result in therapists feeling unqualified to provide services for this vulnerable population. With few exceptions, current literature focuses on the emotional and physical effects of sexual abuse on children but falls short of identifying treatment objectives or strategies. *Choosing to Heal* addresses the effects of child sexual abuse and provides counselors and other psychological professionals with valuable techniques to utilize in their treatment environments.

Choosing to Heal breaks ground as the first resource to use reality therapy/choice theory techniques and concepts in focusing on the treatment of sexually abused children. Reality therapy is based on universal principles and is practiced in many cultures and countries. Choice theory® states that all humans have five basic needs: the need to survive, the need for love and belonging, and the needs for power, freedom, and fun. In this book children and their caretakers are taught choice theory as a part of their counseling process. They learn to identify coping patterns that have been chosen to deal with the aftermath of sexual abuse. Behaviors, cognitive processes, feelings, and physiological responses to sexual abuse are examined. Reality therapy encourages self-evaluation of current acting and thinking behaviors by children and caretakers in order for change to occur in areas of identified difficulty. Choice theory emphasizes that people are not at fault for sexual abuse that has occurred to them; however, they are responsible for how they choose to respond to the abuse. In this way, victims are encouraged to become survivors and avoid self-defeating lifestyles.

Readers of *Choosing to Heal* are provided with numerous strategies that focus on teaching children the new behaviors and thought processes that will help them to heal. These new skills will replace previous coping skills that may have been psychologically or physically harmful to them. Techniques are provided for an age range from preschool to adulthood. Therapists are encouraged to modify these for use within their settings to best serve the children who are their clients. Information and techniques are not gender specific except in the section in chapter 2, "Considerations in the Sexual Abuse of Males." The term *caretaker* is used throughout the book to refer to anyone who directly takes care of children.

Case studies are provided to demonstrate the use of specific techniques or to better define a particular subject area. The names and ages of clients have been altered to protect the confidentiality of the children and families in these examples. Cases will include these:

- The smell of popcorn was the trigger for a 10-year-old girl to self-injure.
- A 15-year-old boy learned he had choices other than fighting to deal with his feeling of anger.
- Two sisters, ages 12 and 13, recanted their abuse but were eventually able to redisclose and testify against their biological father.
- A mother denied her children's abuse but was able to come to terms with the truth through a group for nonoffending parents.
- A 13-year-old girl changed her sexualized behaviors and developed better peer relationships.
- A resistant 6-year-old boy responded to the use of therapeutic humor to develop positive decision making.

In addition to providing mental health professionals with a valuable resource to add to their tool kit, *Choosing to Heal* will benefit an even larger population of readers. Parents, teachers, physicians, childcare providers, and everyone who cares about children and this horrific crime against children can learn how child sexual abuse affects children and how they can contribute, through their own behaviors, to helping children heal.

CHAPTER 1

An Introduction to Choice Theory and Reality Therapy

Things do not change, we do.

Henry David Thoreau

Dr. William Glasser, in his book *Reality Therapy* (1965), rejected the Freudian model of therapy that emphasized a focus on the past and on unconscious thought processes for which the person was not held responsible. The core of reality therapy focuses on an individual's responsibility for his or her own behavior. Glasser's book advanced the position that all problems exist in the present, therefore minimal therapy time should be spent focusing on the past. Choice theory,® also developed by Glasser, provides the foundation for the use of reality therapy techniques and interventions.

The choice theory approach to counseling explains that for all practical purposes, everything people do is a result of the choices they make. This includes an individual's choice to be happy or unhappy. The present book deals with the use of choice theory to treat cases of sexual abuse in children and contends that the response to that abuse is the choice of the individual.

It is only rarely possible to truly control another person's behavior. Choice theory places responsibility on the person, not parents, society, or others, for the choices the person makes in developing the behaviors necessary to survive abuse. These behaviors may not initially seem the most effective or responsible, but they represent children's best attempts to cope at that time. It is never the therapist's job to criticize or judge coping skills.

Counseling with choice theory involves teaching and providing information that helps children cope responsibly with abuse and discontinue self-defeating behaviors. Children who must cope with sexual abuse will choose the most effective behavior that meets or satisfies their basic needs. These behaviors may be influenced by prior learning, available resources, accidental discovery, and by the degree that the new behaviors reduce emotional and physical pain. Choice theory and reality therapy focus on teaching responsible behaviors — those that satisfy basic needs without interfering with the basic needs of others. Choice theory defines the basic needs as survival, love and belonging, power, freedom, and fun.

Reality therapy can be taught and made use of with a wide age range. Preschool and elementary school children are capable of learning choice theory concepts that involve taking responsibility for their choices and the consequences incurred. For example, children who use the behavior of hitting to meet their power need can be asked to take a time-out to self-evaluate their behavior and develop plans for new behaviors. Following this period of time-out, parents and children can discuss behaviors that meet the need for power that do not result in undesirable consequences such as harming relationships with others. Younger children learn best through caregivers who practice choice theory in their parenting and model these behaviors in daily life. Therapists and teachers can incorporate choice theory into their practice and classrooms. The results of these practices are children who thrive, enjoy life, and are resilient in response to life's events.

External control psychology and traditional parenting education is based on the principle that people choose to react because of external stimuli. An example of this is the response to a ringing doorbell. The bell may ring, but it may be answered or ignored. Based on the principles of external control, the ringing bell (external control) is the reason people react. Choice theory, based on the principle of internal control, examines the internal processes and elements of choice that result in the response to the ringing bell. For example, if the person who rings the bell is someone one wants to see, then the choice will probably be to answer the door. However, if one is aware that the person is not someone that one wants to see, then one may choose to pretend that one is not home. When parents or teachers attempt to bribe children to behave in a way that the adults want them to behave, children do not always consider the bribe (external control) valuable enough to warrant a change in behavior. This response on the part of children takes place because they are motivated by internal forces, such as their perceptions about the event, and recognition that they have a choice about their actions.

Sexually abused children do not all react in an identical way to abuse. Their perceptions about the offender, themselves, their support systems, and the actual abuse events all influence their reactions.

Devastating emotional effects can occur when parents and caregivers use external control parenting techniques with sexually abused children. Sexual abuse results in a violation of trust by someone with more power. The child often feels manipulated or coerced into doing what the abuser wants. In an attempt to manage the child's behaviors following the abuse, the caregiver may use external controls such as bribes or threats. These behaviors may be perceived by the child as another attempt to diminish, manipulate, or take away their power. As a result the child's undesirable behaviors may intensify and the relationship between child and caregiver suffers.

Often, people enter therapy because they are in pain as a result of ineffective behavioral or thinking processes. They want to change how they are feeling or their somatic responses to situations. Through choice theory, people learn that they can make changes in themselves, their behaviors, and perceptions that result in more effective ways of meeting the basic needs. Choice theory states that everyone is born with encoded genes that drive all behaviors. These basic needs, as stated earlier, are survival, love and belonging, power, freedom, and fun.

Article I. The Basic Needs of Choice Theory

The need for survival involves food, warmth, oxygen, water, and sleep. As human beings, the need for survival usually takes precedence over psychological needs.

Section 1.01 Survival

Young children are unable to provide for their own survival basics, such as food and water, and are dependent on adults to help them survive. The adults who are responsible for helping children survive are often the same adults who threaten the child's actual or perceived survival through abuse, neglect, and maltreatment. Children rely on their adult caregivers to provide them with a safe environment. When children do not have their basic survival needs met, they may develop fear and uncertainty about their ability to be protected and survive. This may manifest itself through a variety of behavioral coping mechanisms that will be discussed in chapter 2.

Children's ability to thrive emotionally and survive physically following sexual abuse is dependent on many factors including resilience. Resilient children are described as those who successfully adapt in the face of adversity and develop social competence despite exposure to severe stressors.

Some specific behaviors or resiliency factors have been identified that lead young children, youth, and adults to overcome traumatic events. These contain both internal and external factors. Bernard (1991) identified five categories of internal traits that lead to resiliency.

1. *Social competencies:* personal responsiveness, flexibility, empathy, good communication skills, and a sense of humor.
2. *Problem-solving skills:* planning, critical consciousness, imagination, resourcefulness, and initiative.
3. *Autonomy:* positive identity and self-esteem, self-worth and self-efficacy, self-discipline, ability to separate or engage in "creative distancing" from dysfunctional situations and resistance.
4. *Religious/spiritual commitment:* stable belief system, sense of usefulness, or membership in a community.
5. *Sense of purpose and future:* special interests, achievement motivation, educational aspirations, healthy expectations, persistence, and hopefulness.

External factors can also influence resilience. These involve caring and support within the three primary systems of children's worlds: (1) family, (2) school, and (3) community.

Children who already possess some of these internal and external factors are more prepared to deal with the aftermath of trauma. The more resiliency factors available to children as a result of genetics, learned skills, environmental factors, and social supports, the more likely it is that children will be able to cope effectively with the emotional impact of abuse. Counseling sexually abused children can help children become aware of and develop internal traits, which promotes resiliency.

Section 1.02 Love and Belonging

Almost everyone wants to feel connected to other human beings, to want friendship, a sense of belonging, and love. Babies communicate the need for belonging and comfort by crying, cooing, eye contact, and physically reaching out. Through these behaviors, attachments begin to form between children and caregivers, and as a result, children are helped to gain a sense of confidence and self-worth that sets the stage for an understanding of how intimate relationships work. Attachments develop as a result of the behaviors by adults who care for children and their cognitive abilities to understand feelings and relationships with the external world. When their basic needs are met in a nurturing manner, babies form secure attachments. Babies whose caregivers are unresponsive or abusive form anxious attachments.

Crittenden and Ainsworth (1989) provided observations regarding the behaviors of children who did not form secure attachments with a primary caregiver.

- Maltreated children display oppositional behaviors or compulsive compliance.

- Children with anxious attachments may demonstrate behaviors that seem paradoxical, such as avoidance and clinging to the caregiver.
- Abused/neglected children are impaired in their ability to feel secure in their exploration of the environment.
- Socially, maltreated children tend to engage in aggression to a greater extent, demonstrate greater vigilance in interaction with peers, or become victims in peer relationships.
- Maltreated/neglected children are more likely to become loners or socially inept because they have not learned the appropriate social skills from caregivers.

Infants and children are mostly limited to the relationships into which they are born, and this research validates the impact on them of abusive behaviors by primary caregivers. It is critical that they be exposed to loving, need-fulfilling relationships to help foster their emotional and social development. When this does not happen, attachment disruptions may occur (see chapter 4). Healthy attachments can only be achieved in a society where adults take responsibility for their behaviors and have an awareness of how their behavior affects children.

It is difficult to avoid relationships. They are a part of everyday life in families, work, school, friendships, clubs, and all other human activities. Unlike food and water, which must sometimes be sought out, people are a plentiful resource. Therefore, it is not the lack of a resource (people) that interferes with the ability to meet the needs for love and belonging, but the behaviors chosen in attempt to meet those needs. There are many external control behaviors that result in deterioration of relationships. Throughout this book, however, the primary focus will be on eliminating those labeled the Seven Deadly Habits (Glasser, 2002) and encouraging behaviors that create connections. These relationship-strengthening behaviors will be referred to as the Seven Caring Habits (Glasser, 2002).

The Seven Caring Habits involve many behaviors that may initially feel unnatural to those who attempt to use them to replace the Seven Deadly Habits. Commitment to wanting a happier relationship by using these

Table 1.1 Seven caring/deadly habits

Seven caring habits	Seven deadly habits
Supporting	Criticizing
Encouraging	Blaming
Listening	Complaining
Accepting	Nagging
Trusting	Threatening
Respecting	Punishing
Negotiating differences	Bribing or rewarding to control

behaviors can result in a rewarding and healthier relationship. Some people are encouraged to "fake it until you make it," which involves the process of behaving in a particular way until it becomes established as a new habit.

An explanation as to the use of each healthy habit is as follows:

1. *Listen:* Silently focus on the other person's verbal and nonverbal behaviors and avoid the Seven Deadly Habits.
2. *Support:* Believe in another person's abilities, efforts, and the way he or she makes decisions.
3. *Encourage:* Communicate belief in one's attempts at successful need-fulfilling behaviors.
4. *Respect:* Have regard for another's worth and dignity.
5. *Trust:* Have confidence in another's actions that do not result in emotional or physical harm to self or others.
6. *Acceptance:* Value another person's efforts and development of his or her own identity.
7. *Negotiate differences:* Find solutions to differences that result in drawing the other person closer rather than pulling the relationship apart.

Section 1.03 Power

Power is a distinctly human need and the one that is most commonly in conflict with the needs of the individuals or other people's needs. The word power often has negative connotations because of its definition as one person's domination over another (power over). There are many examples of how people gain power at the expense of someone else's power being diminished. These include child abuse cases, domestic violence, boss-managed work environments, and many educational classroom settings. These situations all involve the external control psychology approach to motivating others to do what those in power assume to be the best idea. Parents, partners, bosses, and school systems often attempt to control through the use of the Seven Deadly Habits. These behaviors diminish the personal power of others, which results in feelings of vulnerability, worthlessness, incompetence, and failure. In turn, these people often choose to continue the cycle of seeking power over others to regain their own perceived loss of power. Choice theory encourages the use of the Seven Caring Habits in relationships to develop balances of power, feelings of connectedness and achievement.

Choice theory focuses on another aspect of power, which is the need to feel inner control over one's life (power within). This can be accomplished through behaviors that result in a person's perception of achievement, accomplishment, recognition, importance, leadership, autonomy, and self-worth. The behaviors will be unique to each individual and determined by their interests and skill levels. By helping people find ways to feel empowered through the use of internal control mechanisms (such as creativity, individuality, and personal expression) the drive to meet their needs in ways that conflict with another's needs is reduced.

Section 1.04 Freedom

The need for freedom involves the urge to make choices, for physical mobility and to be internally free. This need is so great that it has invoked wars and people have chosen to die for it. In other situations, people have protested for their rights to read, write, and say what they choose. Freedom is a powerful motivator. However, freedom is often taken for granted until it is threatened.

Relationships, whether between parents and children or two adults, often suffer as a result of the struggle for freedom. Adolescents constantly test the boundaries of freedom and parents typically respond with external controls such as manipulation, coercion, bribery, or punishment to control and limit the adolescent's freedom. The result of this behavior is a power struggle.

Adults also attempt to control and restrict their partner's freedom in order to, in their perception, limit the person from finding another partner. In reality it disconnects the current relationship and increases the chances the partner will look for a new relationship where he or she is not restricted. The result in either situation may be passivity or aggression. Although those behaviors are often used both decrease the strength of the relationship and the happiness of the individuals.

Section 1.05 Fun

Without fun, most people do not identify feeling much happiness or pleasure in life. A valuable part of any relationship involves shared fun activities. Babies and children are encouraged to have fun and enjoy their experiences. But as children enter into adolescence and adulthood this is often discouraged and labeled as immature. School systems and work environments use external controls to discourage behaviors they consider unproductive. Because everyone has the drive to meet the basic need for fun, a child or employee may experience feelings of boredom, apathy, or depressing thoughts that actually lead to a lack of motivation and less productivity. The inability to meet the need for fun effectively may also result in behavioral choices such as seeking negative attention, aggression, skipping school or work, and higher levels of somatic complaints.

Fun is an important part of the learning process. It is a psychological and physiological payoff of learning and the enjoyment that comes from mastering a skill. Children and adults who engage in positive and fun experiences with others are more likely to identify themselves as happy and successful in their undertakings. Cooperative play between children also establishes the opportunity for internal evaluation of whether their behaviors create positive relationships. For example, a 6-year-old boy who is bossy and controlling with his peers may determine his behavior needs modifying unless he wants to be without playmates. Adults, who engage in irresponsible or abusive behavior toward friends, and perceive the behavior as being "all in fun," may also find themselves shunned if they do not evaluate their behaviors and make changes that encourage positive relationships.

In some circumstances, such as sexual abuse, fun is a difficult concept to grasp. Children may spend so much time focused on how to survive their abuse that they may have little emotional or physical energy for fun. Some children also avoid social relationships because of low self-worth. This isolation also prevents the fun associated with peer interaction.

Like all the basic needs, the need for fun can be in direct conflict with the individuals' or other people's needs. For example, a person may consider mountain climbing to be fun, a way to gain a sense of achievement (power), something of their choice (freedom), and doing something enjoyable with others (belonging). However, mountain climbing claims the lives of many people each year and therefore conflicts with the need for survival.

There are varying intensity levels between individuals' basic needs that contribute to individual differences. This is often evident in marriages where, for example, one person has a high need level for freedom and the other does not. Conflict arises when people cannot respect these differences in needs. Another example in relationships is when one person has a high need level for love and belonging combined with low need level for power. In these situations the person may choose a highly charismatic partner who has a high need for power. This combination can create the foundation for an abusive relationship. This combination of need levels may result in difficulty for the partner who wants relationships more than personal power.

Article II. The Quality World

The quality world is made up of positive perceptions of people, situations, and things. These perceptions are often made up of visual images or "pictures." Approximately 80% of the perceptions in the quality world are visual. Perceptions may also be tactile, olfactory, auditory, or gustatory. These pictures identify how people ideally want to satisfy their basic needs. When a person's need is satisfied, then it might be placed in the quality world. This collage of pictures is unique to each individual. Although people may share some common pictures, the overall collection is personal and determined by that person's life experiences. These pictures begin to be collected shortly after birth and continue to be added, removed, or modified throughout the life span. A quality world does not exist as a true snapshot of a situation but is based on the person's perceptions of what he/she has experienced or wants. Examples of perceptions of what is wanted may include the ideal family or mate, career success, physical fitness levels, a desired vacation, or hopes for the future. When a person successfully meets the picture in the quality world, he/she feels satisfied. If the picture is not being met, the person experiences frustration and will be motivated to find a behavior that will reduce the difference between what he/she wants and what currently exists. This does not mean that others always view a quality world picture as the best choice. This is demonstrated by classroom behaviors. Children who do not have school in their quality world may decide to meet their needs for love and belonging by being the class clown or their need for power by being defiant toward the teacher. Despite consequences, these children may continue to meet their needs through negative behaviors unless teachers can find ways to empower them and help place school in their quality world.

Quality pictures are typically specific and clear. Wubbolding (2000) suggested, however, that occasionally pictures can be blurred. He indicated that adolescents and people struggling with addictions or emotional upsets may experience difficulty in clearly identifying what it is that they currently want.

Pictures in the quality world do not have to be rational, they only have to meet that person's basic needs. This occurs with pedophiles when they attempt to meet their needs for love and belonging or power by sexually abusing children and teenagers below the age of consent. Most people would view these behaviors as irrational.

Allen, 38 years old, requested therapy following a disclosure of sexual abuse made against him by his 14-year-old stepdaughter. He admitted to the abuse and was awaiting court hearings and sentencing. He expressed remorse for his actions and identified this as the only sexually abusive act he had ever committed against a child. His biological teenage daughters were all interviewed by child protection services and denied any inappropriate sexual behaviors toward them by their father. He had been married for several years, but he reported little emotional connection between himself and his wife. He also stated he felt worthless because she earned more money than he did. Allen stated that he had always been a loner and had many difficulties with peers as a child. He reported that his stepdaughter was also a loner and he frequently spent time with her because she had few friends. He stated that he gradually began to view their relationship as adult-adult instead of adult-teen. He stated that they shared common interests and had large amounts of time together as a result of his wife's work schedule. He reported that he wanted to take the relationship to the "next level" so he initiated sexual activity. He stated that he sexually abused her for about 6 months and recognized it was inappropriate but did not want to stop because of the happiness he felt as a result of their "special relationship" and emotional connection. Allen reported he was experiencing depression as a result of impending incarceration but also because of the loss of the ability to continue experiencing the relationship that made him feel loved, powerful, and happy.

Allen's picture of his stepdaughter in his quality world as an ideal relationship was not rational. Despite an awareness of the consequences of his actions and the emotional damage on his stepdaughter he continued to view her as fulfilling his needs. Allen was not incarcerated and was instead referred to a sex offenders program to focus on creating behaviors that would more appropriately meet his basic needs. However, it is difficult to remove pictures that are highly satisfying in terms of need. This is one reason treatment of child sexual abuse offenders is a long and difficult process.

It is difficult, but not impossible to remove a picture from the quality world. Consider the pain a person experiences when a once need-fulfilling relationship ceases to result in positive feelings. A person can decide that keeping a picture is too painful and attempt to find a new picture to meet the need for love and belonging. Some may choose to modify the picture and accept the current relationship for what it does provide in meeting their basic needs. Others determine that the only option is to completely remove the picture of the person. A sexually abused child whose offender is also a parent may not want to remove the person from his or her quality world. The youngster may choose to modify their picture of the ideal loving parent to that of a parent who committed an unacceptable act. In circumstances such as pedophilia, offenders who are unable to remove the picture of sexual abuse as need satisfying must choose to either learn ways to cope with the frustration of an unmet quality world picture, and live within the legal expectations of society, or face the consequences of recidivism.

An additional consideration regarding quality world pictures and sexually abused children is pictures that are temporarily or sometimes completely unable to be retrieved. Henry, an adult survivor of childhood sexual abuse, described the following experience.

For years I repressed so many of the memories of my childhood. I don't know if I was just ignoring them, actually forgetting them or refusing to deal with them. But I knew there were "things" that were there in my mind. I knew because of the fears of dark rooms and of the night. I knew because of fear of what might be lurking in the next room, behind a tree, or following me down the street. I knew I had things stored in the attic of my mind but I chose not to open them up or deal with them.

Mixed up with the bad things in my attic were some good things. The good things were memories of Mr. Walters who took me to baseball games at the minor league park in our town. He had no children, but he had box seats right behind home plate and he took me. We had good times. He never hurt me. He never made me scared. Mrs. Janus, the next-door neighbor, knew how I loved to eat and I became her chief food taster. Her grandchildren lived far away and she didn't see them often, so she picked me to like. She never hurt me. She never made me scared.

It was several decades later that I was encouraged to return to my attic and to retrieve my pictures. It made me realize that I was cared for by special people who sensed my loneliness. I don't think they would have ever had an idea why I was so lonely and frightened, but out of kindness, they were havens of safety for me in a very troubled world.

This story demonstrates the power of dissociative processes that protect children from fully experiencing all the emotional and physical pain associated with sexual abuse. Through his attempts to distance himself from his abuse experiences, Henry also temporarily blocked some quality world pictures. These pictures were not removed, only temporarily unavailable due to stress and avoidance of dealing with his sexual abuse. Only when he became an adult and chose to disclose and confront the effects of sexual abuse on his life did he also open the "attic door" to many quality experiences from childhood.

Article III. Total Behavior

From a choice theory standpoint, behavior is made up of four separate components: acting, thinking, feeling, and physiology. These components occur simultaneously; therefore all behavior is total behavior.

1. Acting (i.e., walking, talking, movement of body parts).
2. Thinking — voluntary or involuntary — (i.e., thoughts, learning, problem solving, fantasies, dreams).
3. Feeling (i.e., happiness, anger, excitement, frustration, sadness, fear).
4. Physiology (i.e., headaches, sweating, tension, blood pressure, temperature, adrenaline rushes).

Although all four components operate together, choice theory emphasizes that the only direct control a person has is over the doing and thinking components. The feeling and physiological responses are consistent with the person's behavioral choices and thoughts. Most people seek psychological treatment because they are in emotional pain. The goal of treatment for them is to "feel" better. The person may also identify numerous somatic difficulties that have arisen as a result of stressful situations. The choice theory approach with clients is to have them focus on changing the thoughts and behaviors that are not as effective as they would like them to be and to develop behaviors that better deal with their stressful situations. Choice theory, therefore, states that people are responsible for their choices to be sad, depressed, or angry and can choose behaviors that have different accompanying emotional responses. Several options may be explored with the client, and they include: (1) changing what is wanted; (2) changing the current behaviors to get what they want; and (3) changing what is wanted and developing new behaviors.

Clients can reduce the physical pain they feel by changing how they cope with life situations.

Jamie, a 17-year-old male, was referred by the Juvenile Probation Department for excessive school absences: Jamie reported frequent headaches, irritable bowel syndrome, and fatigue. A physical examination was requested and a medical disorder was ruled out. Jamie described his home life as chaotic with parental domestic violence and alcohol abuse. Jamie stated that some of his school absences were the result of thinking that by staying home he could protect his mother from additional domestic abuse. He stated that it only protected her initially and that his father had recently begun to be physical in his presence too. Despite the frequent school absences Jamie was an A/B student, had several close friends, and was on the football team. Treatment with Jamie consisted of focusing on what he had control over in his life (attending school, getting a part-time job, buying a car, graduating, and the coping behaviors he needed in order to deal effectively with his parents). Jamie began to let go of trying to stop the drinking and fights between his parents, obtained a job, bought a car, focused on his own future, and was determined not to continue the pattern of behavior modeled by his parents. Despite the parents' unwillingness to be directly involved in the treatment process, they supported his decision to work, and helped him buy a reasonably priced car. As Jamie was able to understand his sphere of control he reported fewer somatic complaints and his school attendance increased to an acceptable level.

This case example demonstrates the process of total behavior. By choosing and acting on new behaviors, letting go of unrealistic thinking patterns (that he could stop the abuse of his mother), Jamie experienced less stress and began feeling happier. In addition to fewer consequences for school absence he reported fewer headaches, diminished irritable bowel problems, and more energy.

In summary, choice theory, an internal control psychology, explains why and how we make the choices that determine the course of our lives. It identifies that:

- All behavior is purposeful.
- Behavior is the result of our attempts to meet our innate basic needs including survival, love and belonging, power, freedom, and fun.
- We can only control our own behavior, not that of anyone else.
- All we can give or get from another person is information.
- What happened in the past has everything to do with what we are today; however, we cannot change the past, therefore we must satisfy our basic needs in the here and now.
- We satisfy our needs through the pictures in our quality world.
- All behavior is total behavior and composed of four components: acting, thinking, feeling, and physiology.
- All total behavior is chosen. However, we only have more direct control over the acting and thinking components, whereas we experience feeling and physiology indirectly through how we choose to act and think.

Article IV. Reality Therapy

William Glasser's *Reality Therapy* (1965) was first published following his graduate training. His theory resulted from questioning the basic tenets of conventional psychology. The concepts of reality therapy were developed with his mentor G. L. Harrington and are now practiced worldwide.

William Glasser initially utilized these concepts of reality therapy in the early 1960s, with great success, at the Ventura School for [Delinquent] Girls. He also discovered that veterans responded positively to these techniques during his work at the Veterans Administration Neuropsychiatric Hospital in Los Angeles. He taught staff in both settings how to apply reality therapy and to treat each person in their care with the belief that they were doing the best they could at the time and were capable of learning new behaviors. The result in both settings was that

Table 1.2 Comparison of Freudian psychoanalysis and reality therapy

Freudian Psychoanalysis	Reality therapy
1. Mental illness exists and can be classified through diagnostic evaluation.	1. The concept of mental illness allows individuals to deny responsibility for behavior. Difficulties arise in people's lives from choices they make in meeting their basic needs.
2. Treatment focuses on examining experiences of the past; behavioral changes occur only after resolution of these issues.	2. It is impossible to change the past; therefore treatment examines the current behavioral and thought processes individuals use to cope and fulfill their needs.
3. Change occurs only through understanding unconscious mental conflicts.	3. Emphasis in treatment is on what the client is currently doing and thinking. "Unconscious motivation" is considered another way for clients to deny responsibility for their behavior.
4. Deviant behavior results from mental illness and external factors such as family or society; therefore clients do not need to evaluate their own behavior.	4. Clients are asked to self-evaluate and take responsibility for whether their behavior is morally right or wrong.

the delinquent girls and veterans began to take more responsibility for their own behavior, gained self–respect, and began to meet their needs in ways that did not conflict with those of others or result in negative consequences. From these early successes reality therapy has continued to evolve into use within school systems ("Quality Schools"), work settings ("Lead Management"), and mental health organizations. Additional information on Quality Schools and Lead Management may be obtained through the William Glasser Institute.

Reality therapy utilizes choice theory concepts and helps clients explore basic needs, wants, and total behavior. Using reality therapy techniques provides information that encourages clients to move from dysfunctional patterns of behavior to healthy, need-fulfilling relationships both inter- and intrapersonally. There is an old saying, "You can't love someone until you love yourself." Clients learn to identify their strengths and appreciate themselves for the effort they put into the process of change. Clients learn the process of self-evaluation and examining behaviors they have chosen in an attempt to meet the basic needs. They learn to let go of self-devaluing thought processes and accept that their behavior always represents their best attempt at any time to meet a need. Choice theory states that people can only control their own behavior; therefore, treatment focuses on helping them cease unproductive attempts to control others.

Article V. Therapeutic Environment

The role of the reality therapist is to create a positive, trusting environment that is need fulfilling. This must happen before change will typically occur. Wubbolding (2000) identified several guidelines for establishing a counseling environment that promotes positive change. These are referred to as the ABs (AB = Always Be).

Always Be:

- Courteous
- Determined
- Enthusiastic
- Firm
- Genuine

The therapist should always role-model appropriate behaviors, and therefore be *courteous* when clients are angry, unresponsive, or sarcastic. Clients then have an opportunity to observe positive responses to their own negative behaviors. Being *determined* involves helping clients recognize that situations can get better, while not giving up on the client's possibilities for change. Through an encouraging and optimistic approach, clients will begin to explore new behavioral directions that will produce desirable outcomes. A therapist should display a positive and upbeat *enthusiasm*. Clients do not need to be subjected to a therapist who does not have effective control in his or her own personal life. It is therefore important for therapists to be aware of and manage their personal issues. It is up to therapists to be *firm* and clear with expectations and guidelines such as those regarding payment and reliable attendance at sessions. Identification of boundaries regarding the therapeutic relationship that include phone calls at home or between sessions should also be clearly defined. In addition, therapists should be *genuine* by being honest and straightforward in their relationship with their clients, thereby acting as role-models for clients to show them appropriate and healthy behavior.

A positive counseling environment is the most effective way to teach the Seven Healthy Habits. Therapists who support, listen, encourage, and respect their clients, while avoiding criticism and a judgmental attitude, facilitate a positive relationship in which clients can grow in emotional terms. Therapists, however, should not encourage or allow excuses for client's behaviors, such as not following through with plans or spotty attendance at sessions. Therapists can aid this process by avoiding "why" questions and asking "what" questions. For example, if the therapist asks, "Why are your parents unhappy with you?" the form of the question encourages excuse making and places the importance of what is happening on the parents. In contrast, asking, "What is something you are doing that causes difficulties between you and your parents?" or "How are you contributing to the problem?" places responsibility for the behavior that is occurring on the client's specific actions. It is crucial to teach clients that excuse making only stands in their way of moving toward new and more productive decisions.

Many clients enter therapy with the perception that bad childhood experiences such as abuse, poverty, parental alcoholism, and divorce are to blame for their behaviors. This belief system allows clients to avoid responsibility for their life choices. Reality therapy techniques help clients realize that they are no longer helpless victims, unless they want and choose to continue to view themselves as such. The suffering and pain of these experiences is not minimized. Clients are encouraged to make a choice to stop suffering and choose coping behaviors that empower and strengthen them. Victims of trauma and abuse do not choose the crimes committed against them but they do choose how they cope. Choice theory emphasizes focus on the here and now; therefore when using reality therapy a counselor does not have clients relive the abuse and trauma. Two exceptions of reviewing the past exist when, (1) a client has not told their story before and been supported, or (2) a client wants to verbalize the story in order to deal with shame issues. Care should be taken to avoid having the client become stuck in the past and thus avoid responsibility for their current behaviors.

Additional elements utilized within the counseling relationship that result in a need-fulfilling environment include:

- *Use of humor:* acceptable and age-appropriate humor and story-telling helps reduce stress and promotes fun (see chapter 7 for guidelines on using humor in therapy).
- *Self-disclosure:* Clients often connect positively with the therapist when they perceive their issues are understood on a personal level (see chapter 8 for more information on self-disclosure).
- *Establishment of professional boundaries:* Safe and ethical behaviors by the therapist are necessary for clients to establish trust and not feel victimized (see chapter 8 for more information on ethics).
- *Encouragement of creativity:* Have clients explore various ways to communicate their thoughts and behaviors, such as using art, poetry, or music to allow for individualized approaches to treatment.

Focus on strengths: Have clients identify and build on areas in which they have experienced empowerment.

Table 1.3 Bob Cockrum's Reality Therapy Flow Chart (The top and bottom bands flow around and through all the other elements.)

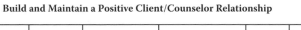

Build and Maintain a Positive Client/Counselor Relationship

Explore wants	Explore behaviors	Make plans
↓	↓	↓
↑	↑	↑

Encourage, ask for, and sometimes share evaluations

Article VI. Procedures and Interventions

Reality therapy helps clients focus on wants, evaluate total behavior, and make commitments to change. Cockrum (1999) established a chart that displays the flow of reality therapy.

The first goal in treatment is to establish rapport and a caring environment with clients. This must occur for the development of trust by clients

Seven Caring Habits	Seven Deadly Habits
Supporting	Criticizing
Encouraging	Blaming
Listening	Complaining
Accepting	Nagging
Trusting	Threatening
Respecting	Punishing
Negotiating differences	Bribing or rewarding to control

Fig. 1.1 Seven habits chart.

WANT　　　　　　HAVE

Fig. 1.2 Balanced scales (satisfaction, no behavioral/perceptual change necessary).

WANT   HAVE

Fig. 1.3 Unbalanced scales (frustration, behavioral/perceptual change is necessary for satisfaction).

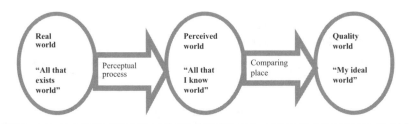

Figure 1.4 The perceptual process.

so that the examination of the quality world "wants," behaviors, and plan development can begin. This atmosphere of trust is to be maintained throughout the therapy process in order for change to occur. In addition, therapists encourage, ask for, and sometimes share their evaluations during the client's exploration of wants, behaviors, and plan making.

A popular reality therapy intervention to help clients understand how wants and behaviors interact is to discuss "scales" and weighing what clients want against the perception of what they have. The scales signal the person as to whether a change in behavior is needed.

Perceptions are each person's internal reality. They are the information from which each person operates. These are processed through "filters" of sensory systems, available knowledge, cultural influences, and values or held beliefs. A perception of what a person wants is then weighed against awareness of what they have. People then choose behaviors to get the desired perception. For example, politicians speak the words we hear. A person assigns a value to the politician that is positive, negative or neutral. Even though the politician says the same words, they can be interpreted differently by separate individuals. The person's perceptions then influence their voting behavior.

Questions are a valuable way to obtain information about what exists in the client's quality world. Through this process the therapist helps clients identify, clarify, prioritize, and evaluate their pictures. Identifying the client's *wants* is crucial in the questioning process.

1. What do you want?
   - in your relationships (spouse, partner, children, family, friends, coworkers)
   - for yourself
   - in your career/education process
     - financially
     - intellectually
   - from therapy
2. If you could change one thing what would it be?
3. How do you want things to be?
4. What would make you happy?
5. What do you *not* want?

Questions are also useful in obtaining information about *total behavior* and *perceptions.*

1. What are you doing to get what you want?
2. What are you being accused of?
3. What are your thoughts when you do that behavior?
4. How do you feel when that is happening?
5. What are your body signals when you do that?

Evaluation questions come by noncritically helping clients review their behaviors for effectiveness.

1. Is this how you want to feel?
2. Did that help you get what you wanted?
3. How is what you are doing helping?
4. Is it helping to look at things that way?
5. Is it possible to get what you want?

During the *plan-making* process the therapist, with permission from the client, may suggest options that can be considered. This is sometimes necessary when clients are having difficulty generating effective behaviors. Questions can also be useful to help clients develop a plan for new behaviors and thought processes.

1. Are you willing to try something different to feel better?
2. What is one thing you can do to improve the situation?
3. What other choices can you make?
4. Is there another way of handling the situation?
5. What knowledge or skills will you need to accomplish this goal?
6. What will not help you meet your goal?

An effective plan should meet several criteria, which includes being simple, realistic, independent of others, action oriented, and immediate.

- *Simple:* Begin with something small and build up. This helps avoid discouragement through gradual achievements.
- *Realistic:* Explore whether the cognitive and physical resources are available for success.
- *Independent of others:* Focus is on the "doer," not others, to change behaviors.
- *Action oriented:* Changes in behaviors need to be identifiable or measurable.
- *Immediate:* Requires implementation right away.

An effective plan is also reviewed for its impact on others. The client can evaluate his or her plan by asking:

1. Is what I want going to harm another person?
2. Will my behavior prevent another person from meeting his or her needs or be in conflict with that person's needs?

Following the establishment and commitment to a plan the client is asked to implement it. In some cases the client may want to rehearse the plan in the therapy setting to feel comfortable carrying it out. Following this process the client is asked to carry through on executing the plan. When requested, the client may set up additional sessions to discuss:

1. *Follow through:* Did the person attempt to do the plan?
2. *Outcome:* Were the desired results obtained?
3. *Modification:* Does the plan require re-evaluation?

Through the process of asking questions, therapists encourage clarification of wants, examination of total behavior, evaluation of current behavior effectiveness, and establishment of plans regarding the situation clients report are causing frustration or pain. It is important to carefully gauge the quality of answers and clients' reactions to the questions. Remember that it is also important to maintain a positive therapeutic relationship or clients may perceive excessive questioning as intrusive and react defensively.

Article VII. Summary

Choice theory and reality therapy principles set the foundation for a new approach to the treatment of sexually abused children. Therapists can use these concepts to help children cope with their victimization by introducing the power of choice in their healing. Child sexual abuse is a horrendous crime that, with a loving and encouraging support system, children can emerge survivors from.

CHAPTER 2

Sexual Abuse and Coping Mechanisms

Our greatest natural resource is the minds of our children.

Walt Disney

The clinical definition of sexual abuse can vary from culture to culture or even within different research studies. In this book, sexual abuse is defined as the use of a child, in a sexual manner, by someone of greater power. The power may be a result of differences in age, size, or mental status; it may be physical, verbal, or emotional. It involves noncontact and contact behaviors by the offender. Noncontact sexual abuse may involve exhibitionism, voyeurism, sexual talk, or exposure to pornography. Contact behaviors include fondling, oral sex, masturbation, intercourse, or anal penetration. Other sexually abusive situations involve child prostitution, exploitation, and involvement in pornography. Regardless of what type occurs, every case of child sexual abuse affects a child and should not be minimized.

Article I. Clinical Studies

Research indicates that child sexual abuse is an alarming problem. The U.S. Department of Health and Human Services (2000) reported that there were an estimated 89,000 substantiated reports made for child sexual abuse. Some studies in the United States have suggested that 20 to 40% of women and 10 to 20% of men were sexually victimized as children (Finkelhor, 1994). Child sexual abuse occurs across all ethnic groups. In a 1994 survey, 44.8% of African-American women, 38% of Caucasian women,

25.6% of Latinas, and 21.1% of Asian-American women reported histories of child sexual abuse (Urquiza & Goodlin-Jones, 1994).

The Australian Institute of Health and Welfare (2003) reported an annual substantiated sexual abuse rate of .9 per 1,000 children in 2001 and 2002. Because substantiated is defined as "proven" in child welfare standards, this number does not include unsubstantiated reports, cases that were recanted or never disclosed. Smallbone and Wortley (2001) surveyed jailed sex offenders. Because participants in the study were given anonymity, they reported that the offenders disclosed only 40% of the child sexual abuse offenses they committed. The offenders reported having committed offenses against 1,010 children (748 males and 262 females). These researchers reported that chronic offenders were more likely to abuse males. One Australian study estimated that 28% of Australian girls and 9% of Australian boys had been involved in some sort of sexual exploitation by an older person (Goldman & Goldman, 1988). MacMillan and associates (1997) reported, in the Ontario Health Survey Supplement, that 4.3% of males and 12.8% of females reported unwanted sexual acts before their 17th birthday. The Badgley Report (1984), using a broader definition of child sexual abuse, obtained a higher prevalence rate. In this study, 31% of boys and 54% of girls under the age of 21 reported sexual abuse. In the Ontario Health Survey Supplement, respondents were asked to indicate whether an adult had committed any of the following acts while they were growing up: "exposed themselves to you more than once; threatened to have sex with you; touched the sexual parts of your body; tried to have sex with you or sexually attacked you."

In the Badgley report, respondents were asked whether any unwanted sexual acts had ever been committed against them and provided a series of items to pick from including unwanted touching of sexual areas and attempted or achieved intercourse.

Julich (2002) studied the economic impact that child sexual abuse had in New Zealand. Her report stated that in New Zealand, 8,600 children are sexually abused for the first time every year, which accounts for 25% of the female population and 9% of the male population being sexually abused before the age of 16. The study stated that adults molested as a child disclose less than 8% of the time. It also reported that child sex offenders average 50 victims before being caught.

The National Commission of Inquiry into the Prevention of Child Abuse in England (2005) reported 2,800 cases of child sexual abuse on their records for the year 2003 to 2004. Placing a name on a child register in England is a measure taken when a child is considered to be at a continued risk of being significantly harmed and in need of a child protection plan. These figures should not be interpreted as an exact figure of child sexual abuse because cases where family support or protection was adequate were not included in the registration.

The actual number of child sexual abuse cases is most likely underestimated because of the inability to determine the numbers that go unreported. Variations in how statistical information is obtained also result in research studies forming different conclusions. Studies differ in which population is studied, such as children or the information obtained from adults regarding their childhood experiences. Other studies research case records, perform telephone interviews, use questionnaires, and may include or exclude noncontact behaviors by offenders. It is also possible that males underreport if words such as *victim* or *abuse* are used when asking whether they have experienced sexual abuse.

Regardless of actual statistical numbers, it is apparent that child sexual abuse is a problem faced by many families and many countries. Children and their families, however, can heal from child sexual abuse, and therapy can be a valuable asset in aiding this process.

Section 1.01 Assessing the Effects

The effects of sexual abuse on the survivor and the coping mechanisms chosen vary significantly from individual to individual. Victimization is an act, by another person of greater power, using his or her position of authority or power to sexually abuse a child. Traumatization can occur when the victim has difficulty coping with the abusive situation both in emotional and behavioral terms. Traumatization is not experienced by every victim of sexual abuse but instead is based on the child's perception of what is occurring and the presence of other factors. These include, but are not limited to:

1. *Duration of the abuse:* The longer the abuse goes on the greater the probability of traumatization. Abusers often escalate from noncontact to contact behaviors, as they become aware that a child is under their control and will not disclose.

2. *Age of child:* Children from birth to age 3 may experience more separation anxiety and fearful reactions. Preschool and elementary age children may display anger, regressive behaviors, and sexual acting out. Preadolescents' and teenagers' responses are more a result of life experiences and exposure to different behaviors.

3. *Relationship/closeness to the offender:* Greater confusion is created when the offender has a close relationship with the victim and a violation of trust has occurred. Roesler and Wind (1994) identified the perpetrator in child sexual abuse of females as follows: 53% being abused by biological fathers, 15% by stepfathers, and 8.8% by uncles.

4. *Presence or absence of support:* Following disclosure, it is important for children to be provided with a safe and caring environment in which to process their sexual abuse issues. Support by nonoffending parents is especially critical to the recovery and healing process. Counselors can also be supportive by helping child sexual abuse victims and their caretakers learn how to cope effectively.

5. *Belief or disbelief:* It is crucial for people in the child's quality world to believe his or her allegations of abuse. Children who are not believed often will not attempt to disclose again. This increases the probability that they will develop behavioral coping mechanisms that interfere with daily functioning and relationships.

6. *Use of force or aggression:* The perception of danger to children's survival results in the possibility of traumatization. The longer the abuse occurs and as children enter adolescence, abusers are more likely to use force or threats of aggression to control children in order to prevent them from disclosing. This is because older children may not respond as easily as younger children to emotional coercion. Also, male victims as compared to female victims are more likely to be seriously injured or die as a result of sexual abuse (Sedlak & Broadhurst, 1996).

7. *Pleasurable experiences during the abuse:* Feelings of shame and self-blame can increase when children experience pleasure during the sexual abuse. Children may believe that the abuse, since pleasurable, must have been wanted on some level. The confusion and shame created results in a lower probability of disclosure.

8. *The presence of other negative life experiences:* When children are also experiencing other negative life factors such as lack of success in school, poverty, divorce, racism, or organic disabilities, they may have more difficulty coping with the sexual abuse.

Article II. Coping Behaviors

In an initial assessment, the counselor will review the child's experience and discuss the continuum of victimization to traumatization both with children, when age appropriate, and caretakers. In addition, the Child Sexual Abuse Assessment Form (see appendix) is reviewed with the child and caretakers to discuss the various cognitive and behavioral coping behaviors used by children referred to counseling.

Minimizing occurs when children, caretakers, offenders, or others indicate through statements or nonverbal behaviors that the abuse was not harmful for a child or family. For example, one family reported that during an interview by a detective, he commented to the parents, "You're really lucky that it only involved fondling and she wasn't raped." This family did not feel "lucky" and was offended and angry about the minimization of their child's experience. Therapists and others need to be aware of how their reactions may further traumatize children or their caretakers.

Attempts to excuse the abuser's behavior are called *rationalizations*. Common rationalizations include, "he was drunk/high," "she was depressed/lonely," and "he was an abused child." In incest cases, rationalization of the mother's choice not to protect her children may occur. This includes, "She was a victim of the offenders too," "She couldn't financially support her children on her own," and "She didn't have support systems." While these conditions may exist, it does not excuse the mother's choice not to protect her children who were incapable of protecting themselves.

Children and caretakers may believe *denial* of the abuse is easier than making a decision to do something different. The choice to deny abuse occurs more often when children have a close relationship with the abuser and have difficulty understanding that the abuser is capable of both loving and abusing them. Mothers may also choose denial when they believe they cannot provide financially for their children if the abuser is moved out of the home or incarcerated. Also, if children are afraid that they may be harmed it is less stressful to deny the abuse than to think about the possibility of being killed.

An 8-year-old girl reported to her therapist that she convinced herself that the abuse was actually a mixture of bad dreams and her overactive imagination. The abuse was discovered when the child tested positive for chlamydia and was asked about sexual contact. She disclosed abuse by a 16-year-old neighbor boy who also tested positive for the infection. She reported that the boy had her witness his killing a cat and told her he would do the same to her and her family if she told anyone about the abuse.

Dissociation allows children to "numb" or distance themselves from emotional or physical pain. In its extreme form children may create separate personalities to "experience" the abuse. Dissociation is not a coping behavior that can be turned on when it is needed and turned off when it is not. For this reason children who attend school may be labeled daydreamers or unmotivated when in dissociative states (see chapter 5 for techniques to use with dissociative reactions). Dissociation also interferes with interpersonal relationships because it can prevent children from experiencing intense emotions such as love or happiness. Any intense feeling can seem overwhelming and this can result in dissociative processes taking place.

Sexual abuse and stress can both result in medical difficulties and somatic pain that requires medical attention. Sexually abused children may also try to draw attention to their emotional hurts through *medical-attention-seeking behaviors* in order to have others focus on real or fabricated physical hurts. They attempt to gain attention for their pain without having to disclose the real reason they are hurting. These children over time may be dismissed as negative attention seekers or hypochondriacs. A positive response to this type of behavior is to state, "I am sorry you are in pain," and then teach the child that they have some choices about how to cope with pain in their lives.

Hyper-alertness develops as children attempt to protect themselves from abusive incidents reoccurring. It can involve being superaware of what is occurring around them such as smells, sounds, others' moods or behaviors, or situations that may indicate the abuse is about to happen again. Unfortunately it usually doesn't protect children long term because the abuser will change strategies to adapt to the thwarted attempts. Children may develop elaborate plans in their attempts to prevent revictimization. In these situations they decide to take an active role in coping with their abuser in order to feel more in control.

Wendy, aged 16, described her attempts to protect herself from further sexual abuse by her older brother's friend who lived with her family. She kept a wind-up alarm clock in her room and when she heard him approaching at night she would quickly wind up the clock and let it ring. He would quickly leave her room to avoid being caught by her parents. She reported becoming a light sleeper after the abuse started in order to try to avoid his sexual abuse.

Children may attempt to stay busy so they have limited opportunities for unwanted thoughts. *Busyness* can help children avoid feeling sad, scared, ashamed, or confused. However, children may be labeled as being hyperactive or having attention-deficit disorder as a result of these attempts to stay constantly busy. It is not unusual for children during high activity phases to be misdiagnosed during psychological evaluations.

Children may attempt to overcompensate for feeling worthless, "broken," and ashamed through *perfectionism*. They believe that through high achievement others will not see the "internal badness." These children may be hesitant to try new things due to fear about whether they can excel. This coping mechanism is unfortunately often overlooked and children can be perceived as coping effectively.

Mental illness can be chosen. It occurs when children determine that they have limited control over what is occurring in the real world and make a decision to create behaviors such as hallucinations or delusions that they do have control over. Glasser (1984) referred to this as "crazy creativity." He defined crazy creativity as anything someone does that people who are "sane" would judge to be unsuitable behavior in a similar situation.

As mentioned previously, under the coping mechanism of seeking medical attention, children may choose to cope with emotional pain by drawing attention to physical hurts they identify themselves as experiencing. Children also develop *self-injurious behaviors* to cope with emotional pain. These behaviors may include cutting themselves with knives or razor blades, eraser-burning the skin, picking sores, pulling out hair on their bodies, or intentionally burning themselves. There is a highly significant relationship between childhood sexual abuse and various forms of self-harm later in life such as suicide attempts, cutting, and self-starving particularly (van der Kolk, Perry, & Herman, 1991). Children choose self-injury behaviors because these behaviors can serve various purposes.

1. Physical damage incurred validates that they are hurting.
2. Physical pain temporarily distracts from the emotional pain.
3. When observed by others it draws attention to their pain.

Drugs and alcohol cause the brain to feel happy or relaxed. Sexual abuse results in feelings of sadness or anxiety. Children with few support systems and unable to find a way to cope positively with emotional pain may choose drugs to alter emotional states to a happier or less anxious level. It may also serve the purpose of inclusion (love and belonging) in a group that also chooses drugs and alcohol in an attempt to meet their psychological needs. Other *addicting behaviors* such as gambling or compulsive sex may also temporarily alter the brain chemicals to produce feelings of intense excitement or pleasure. Because these feelings are temporary, children must constantly repeat these behaviors to obtain the results they desire.

Children who are violated sexually by someone they know and trust may determine it is not safe to trust anyone, including their own perceptions about contact with other people. As a result they may choose to isolate and *avoid intimate relationships*. The perception is that, "If I don't let anyone get close, I can't get hurt."

Eating-disordered behaviors, such as anorexia and bulimia are another way children choose to feel in control of their bodies. The abuse may result in the belief by children that they do not have a choice about what is done to their body. The bingeing and purging is a way of taking control over what does or does not go in (food) or out (purging). They discover that it is difficult for anyone else to control when, what, and how much they eat.

Children may also limit food intake to avoid physical maturity, which they believe will be attractive to an abuser. Even under conditions such as hospitalization, children often become creative and remove feeding IVs and hide or throw away food. Attempts to control these behaviors to "cure" children by forcing, criticizing, or bribing them to gain weight can result in increased resistance so they can maintain feelings of power and control.

Abuse teaches children directly and indirectly to lie. Offenders may tell children not to tell anyone and to lie if asked about sexual abuse. Children may decide to maintain secrecy to protect the abuser, themselves, or the family and then lie to others about physical or emotional problems. Over time *lying* can become a natural behavior for abused children and they may begin to lie about other areas of their lives that are not directly connected to the abuse. As a result, attempts to disclose at some point may result in people judging that the abuse is another lie. It is important for children's disclosures to always be taken seriously, even when there is a history of lying.

Shoplifting and theft excites children and provides a distraction, at that moment, from emotional pain and intrusive thoughts. The act of stealing requires children to be focused on the activity, thereby providing relief from concerns about the abuse. These feelings of excitement are temporary and therefore must be repeated over and over to recreate the desired effects.

Michael, 12 years old, was referred after his mother discovered her teenage stepson was forcing Michael to perform oral sex on him. Michael reported to the therapist that the abuse had been occurring almost daily for 6 months. A review with Michael of his coping behaviors resulted in his discussing his shoplifting, which had started about 1 month after the abuse began. He described feeling "great" when he stole items, even if they were things he did not want or threw away later. He said that he would shoplift almost every time he was in a store and had also begun to steal when he was at the homes of friends and family. He stated he wanted to stop before he was caught but was feeling stronger urges to steal and had begun to fantasize about breaking into a neighbor's home.

Sometimes children *sexually act out* toward peers, younger children, adults, and animals. This act helps reposition their role from a powerless position (victim) to powerful (sexual acting out). If physical pleasure is experienced during the abuse some children try to re-create this by engaging others in a similar sexual act with them (see chapter 7 for more information about sexual acting out). Older sexually abused children may discover that sexualized behaviors gain them attention that they perceive as love/belonging.

Fire setting can be a powerful experience for a sexual abuse victim. Fire and its destruction can result in feelings of control, excitement and power.

Randy, 16 years old, a sexual abuse victim, described numerous incidents of arson. He identified his abuse as beginning at age 5 and lasting 5 years. His paternal uncle was the offender. The uncle was sent to prison on charges of molestation of a female child in the family but no one ever inquired about Randy being victimized. Randy told the therapist that his discovery of fire setting and how much he felt energized by it began when he was 5 or 6 years old. He said it began with wastebasket fires for a couple of years and that his family wasn't overly concerned, and even jokingly called him a "little pyromaniac." He said that his fire setting progressed from junkyard fires, to cornfields, then barns. At the time of referral Randy was serving time in a residential youth facility for arson. He disclosed the sexual abuse when a therapist he had formed a trusting relationship with asked him if he had ever been touched in a sexual way that he did not consent to or felt confused about.

Anger can be harmful and be directed inward through self-blame or outward by lashing out verbally or physically. Sexually abused children who are unable or unwilling to lash out at the abuser or those who did not protect them may choose to lash out at those closest to them. This can include people such as peers, loving caretakers, teachers, and therapists. These reactions of anger occur toward people with whom they feel most safe and trust not to react with abusive behavior. Nonoffending parents and caretakers often express confusion when they find they are the objects of children's anger. Helping them reframe this as an indication that trust has developed with them may help relieve some of the stress they are experiencing. Part of the therapy process will involve helping children learn how to direct anger at the appropriate sources in a way that does not cause harm to them or their relationships.

During and after the abuse, children may begin clinging to people they perceive can protect them and demonstrating *separation anxiety*. They may become fearful when left in previously comfortable environments such as school, sports, or anywhere they think that it is possible to encounter an abusive situation. Even teenaged children may be afraid to sleep or remain alone in the home. This demonstrates the effect sexual abuse has on children's sense of security and survival.

Child sexual abuse victims may develop a *preoccupation with sex and masturbation*. Younger children whose sexual knowledge is escalated by sexual abuse may become hyperaware of sexual undertones and overtones in movies, magazines, and the actions of others. Masturbation may also become frequent and be used as a way to cope whenever children experience confusing emotions such as fear, anger, or are under stress.

Unfortunately, children may decide that there is no way to end the abuse or emotional pain resulting from the abuse and choose *suicide* as their coping mechanism. This choice tends to increase in probability as traumatization factors increase. A child who contemplates suicide usually expresses intense loneliness and feelings of isolation. At the point this coping behavior is chosen, it is rare for them to report that they believe any of their basic psychological needs are being met. Children often give up hope, believing they are unable to satisfy any quality world pictures.

Children do not always experience traumatization from child sexual abuse and may only want to focus on concerns about behavioral choices they recognize that they have control over. Sherry was an example of this type of case. She had received support and protection from many people, including her mother, child social services, extended family, and her offending father.

Sherry, 13 years old, was referred to a therapist by the state social service agency, for sexual abuse by her biological father. Sherry disclosed the sexual abuse to her mother, who immediately contacted the police, and asked the father to leave the home. This belief, protection, and support by her mother provided Sherry with relief from the anxiety and fear she had been experiencing about whether to disclose. In addition, Sherry's father confessed and promised not to go to trial with the case in order to avoid Sherry having to testify. Despite her father being the offender, Sherry continued to perceive him as loving and concerned about her. Sherry also developed a close and connected relationship with the therapist and therefore worked diligently on the behaviors that she had been choosing that were causing difficulties for her. These behaviors included low motivation toward schoolwork, isolating from peers, and fatigue.

Many children do not receive the support needed to cope positively with the abuse. This occurred in the case of Misty.

Child protection services (CPS) referred Misty, 5 years old, because of sexual abuse by her stepfather. Misty had been raised by her maternal grandparents from birth due to her mother's incarceration, but had recently returned to the care of her biological mother and stepfather. The mother stated she believed her own parents coached the disclosure in an attempt to have Misty returned to them. She agreed to have the stepfather move out pending an investigation of the sexual abuse. The maternal grandparents were also denied unsupervised visitation during the investigation. Misty and her mother appeared together at the intake. Misty appeared withdrawn and sat next to the therapist instead of her mother. She avoided eye contact with the mother and flinched when the mother moved toward her. The mother described Misty as a "horrible child who wet herself, smeared feces on the wall, and refused to behave." The mother refused to allow the therapist to talk with Misty alone stating they were ordered for "family therapy." The grandparents were seen at a separate session and described Misty as a loving child who had been toilet trained since 2 ½ years old. They expressed concern that Misty had been taken from the only home and parents she had ever known and returned to a mother who had a history of drug addiction and emotional problems. They also stated they had observed and photographed bruises on Misty's body at a recent visit yet CPS believed the story the mother provided about the bruises. The grandparents believed Misty's recent behavior problems were a result of abuse occurring in her mother's home. A series of medical tests revealed both physical and sexual abuse, which the mother refused to believe were inflicted by her own husband. This case reflected the devastating emotional effects that sexual and physical abuse can have on a child's behaviors. Caregivers and family, with the exception of her mother, had observed Misty prior to her return to the biological mother's care, to be a loving and carefree child with normal developmental patterns. Following placement into an abusive environment, Misty began to display regressive and out of control behavior to cope with the trauma she was experiencing.

Assessment of trauma factors can help therapists understand whether children have the cognitive abilities or support systems available to help them heal from sexual abuse. Children are able to learn that, while their coping skills may not be viewed positively by others or caused undesirable consequences, they did the best they could at that time. Child sexual abuse is not an excuse for misbehavior. Children can learn and choose new coping behaviors.

Article III. Considerations in the Sexual Abuse of Males

Like females, male children cope with child sexual abuse through a variety of behaviors. However, males may also experience issues related to differences resulting from societal expectations in males and perceptions about male child sexual abuse. For the most part society discourages helplessness in males, which is an inherent trait in sexual abuse. These issues with helplessness and powerlessness will often result in boys becoming bullies at school (see chapter 6 for more information on bullying) or being bullied. In this latter situation, bullies may target males who become withdrawn and appear vulnerable. This sets up scenarios for repeated victimization and additional emotional difficulties.

Boys may be hesitant to disclose their sexual abuse because they may be concerned about their masculinity being questioned. Males are expected to be "macho," to not feel powerless, to always be in control, and to not be vulnerable under any circumstances (Hunter, 1990). These messages are sent early to male children by families and society through statements such as "suck it up," "be tough," "don't act like a sissy," and "be a man." Whenever they encounter physical or emotional pain and distress, these signals set the stage for fewer disclosures by males who are victimized. Because their feelings of emotional vulnerability are not socially acceptable, many males will choose expressions of anger to vent these emotions. Therefore, counseling needs to address the effectiveness of the males' coping decisions in the areas of vulnerability, helplessness, fear, and dependency. These feelings may be masked by overcompensation behaviors such as cockiness, aggression, or risk taking. Male children believe these behaviors will mask their internal concerns about their masculinity.

Confusion about sexuality and sexual orientation can develop following male child sexual abuse.

When pleasurable feelings are elicited during sexual abuse by male sexual offenders, boys may be concerned about being or labeled as homosexual. In an attempt to reduce their fears about homosexuality or prevent others from perceiving them as homosexual, some males develop homophobia, an irrational fear or intolerance of homosexuality (Gilgun & Reiser, 1990). They may take desperate measures as teens and young adults to prove to themselves and to others that they are not gay. Common behaviors include acting macho, having multiple female sexual partners, trying to get a woman pregnant, or harassing gay men (Munro, 2000).

It is important to address with male children whether these concerns are present. It is critical to help males, like females, understand that their bodies are made to respond physiologically to stimulation and a physically pleasurable response does not mean they wanted to be abused or are homosexual. This can help reduce the shame and self-blame many male child abuse victims would not otherwise bring up. Males, without a caring male figure in their lives, may also assign guilt to themselves when they wanted the nonsexual aspects of the relationship. Therapists can help males understand that wanting to bond with an adult male whom they admire or initially want to emulate does not give that adult the right to misuse the trust they have been given by the child.

Boys molested by female offenders may be confused about feeling violated and powerless when their experience is labeled as "getting lucky" by others or was pleasurable. It is rare to hear about female children being congratulated when an adult introduces them to sex through sexual activities; however, males are often praised for being "initiated" into adulthood by an adult female. It is a widely, and wrongly held belief that boys often initiate the sexual contact they have with adults and that these contacts do not negatively affect boys (Finkelhor, 1984.) This is supported by research that indicates that sexually abused boys are more likely to have problems with substance abuse (Krug, 1989), suicide attempts (Briere & Runtz, 1986), eating disorders (Neumark-Sztainer, Story, Hannan, Beuring, & Resnick, 2000), intimacy and peer relations (Lisak, 1994), trust (Dimock, 1988), and negative self-beliefs (Matthews, 1996).

Another wrongly held belief, associated primarily with male sexual abuse victims, is that they will become sex offenders. There is no valid research that supports this belief. In fact, many male sex offenders do not have a history of being sexually abused as children (Garland & Dougher, 1990). Sex offenders more often grew up in families where they suffered from other forms of abuse such as physical and emotional abuse. Therefore, sexual victimization in childhood does not automatically result in sexually aggressive behaviors in adulthood. Sex offenders do have higher than expected rates of sexual abuse in their histories, but the majority were not sexually abused as children (Becker & Murphy, 1998).

Some additional differences identified in research literature point out some predominately male concerns as compared to females.

- Boys appear more likely than girls to be abused by multiple perpetrators (Crowder, 1995).
- Male victims and their parents are more likely to minimize the impact of child sexual abuse (Finkelhor, 1984).
- Male sexual abuse victims are more likely than females to abuse drugs as a coping behavior (Holmes & Slap, 1998).
- Male children are more likely to be sodomized during sexual abuse (Crowder, 1995).

This information regarding male sexual abuse victims will alert therapists that not only do individual differences exist between sexual abuse victims but that gender differences also should be acknowledged when considering how sexual abuse victims cope. Helping male children, as well as females, understand the effects of child sexual abuse, and how their current behaviors reflect their best attempts to cope, sets the stage for healing.

Treatment utilizing reality therapy emphasizes the importance of children learning new coping behaviors and thought processes that will more effectively meet the basic needs identified in choice theory.

Choice theory teaches that all of our behavior is generated to satisfy five genetically driven needs.

Article IV. Meeting the Basic Needs after Sexual Abuse

Sexual abuse can result in (1) a person's perception that his or her life is in danger, and (2) a person's choice of coping behaviors that are a threat to the basic need for survival.

Section 4.01 Survival

Children may fear for their lives and choose not to disclose as a result of physically painful sexual abuse or threats to prevent them from reporting abuse. In an attempt to do the best they can at the time, children may choose behaviors that are dangerous to their survival such as self-mutilation, suicide, sex, or drug abuse. The threat of suicide should always be immediately addressed and steps taken to protect children from intentional or accidental death. Also children must be provided with safety from revictimization, and their environment needs should be assessed for the ability to provide this. In many cases, children, despite legal involvement, will continue to have contact with the offender or others who will attempt to have them recant the abuse. It is important in these cases to develop strong collaborative relationships with the social service agencies and court systems. This serves the purpose of protecting children by sharing information between the support services and reducing the likelihood of children slipping through the cracks.

Section 4.02 Love and Belonging

From the time children are born they behave in ways that enable their basic needs to be met. For example, a baby cries when hungry or soiled. If this behavior is met by loving caretakers, these individuals become a part of that child's quality world. For children, these relationships begin to establish an early behavioral pattern that meets the needs for survival, love, and belonging. In his attachment theory approach to early childhood experiences and relationship building, Bowlby (1969/1982) postulates that there is a universal need to form close affectional bonds. If the needs of children are met and reciprocated by attachment behaviors such as holding, comforting, or rocking, then these behaviors strengthen the attachment bonds between children and caregivers.

Consider what occurs to children's thought process after they have been sexually abused. Children may perceive the offender as a loving parent or caretaker and also as someone who violated them. They will have pictures of people in their quality world that they expected to believe, support, and protect them. When this doesn't happen, conflict is created between what they want to occur and reality. Children may struggle with issues such as fear of intimate relationships, separation anxiety, or poor boundaries with others. As a result, creative thinking and behavioral mechanisms to reduce the cognitive dissonance develop (see chapter 4 for more information on attachment disruptions). A part of the therapeutic process will be to help children form healthy responses to cope with their sexual abuse.

Lana, age 12, and Laura, age 13, were referred after Laura told a friend at school that her father had been having sex with both Laura and her younger sister, sometimes together. The friend told the school counselor who contacted child protection services (CPS). The CPS then came to school, interviewed both girls, placed them in protective custody, and took them to a local group home. The girls separately provided information about numerous incidents of sexual abuse by their biological father who lived with them, along with their mother and 17-year-old brother. Both also reported that they had told the mother about the abuse and she had said, "Just stay away from him." When interviewed by the CPS worker, the mother labeled Laura as "a trouble-making, lying, slut." The mother stated the younger daughter had probably been manipulated by her sister to say she had also been abused. The mother stated she believed that the motivation behind the sexual abuse statements was an attempt to get back at their father for being too strict. After discovering that the mother did not believe them and was not going to ask the father to leave the home, the girls recanted the abuse so that they could return home. The girls were returned home but the courts maintained temporary wardship. The family was mandated to undergo individual and family treatment. Within one month, Laura redisclosed to her therapist and also reported she planned to commit suicide, therefore child protection services was contacted to collaborate on treatment. The girls asked to be interviewed at the therapist's office and this request was granted. The therapist then accompanied Laura for an inpatient evaluation due to her claims of planning to commit suicide. The therapist also helped Lana during her move to a protective group home. Laura was also allowed to maintain regular contact with her outpatient therapist during her inpatient treatment. Upon Laura's release from the inpatient facility, she returned to outpatient counseling. The mother also returned to treatment to focus on her relationship with the girls.

Many people question why children would recant when they realize that they are going to return to an abusive environment. If one examines the process with choice theory, the explanation becomes clear. In this case, as in many others, the mother, father, and an intact family unit is a part of the children's quality world. At the time of the initial disclosure, Laura wanted to make the sexual abuse end but had been unable to achieve this on her own. Her chosen behavior to reduce the difference in her "scales" was to disclose. The disclosure did not get her what she wanted and the "scales" did not balance. Laura and Lana realized they would not get what they wanted if they stuck to their story because their mother did not plan to support the disclosure or believe them; therefore they could not return home to her. The mother and an intact family were in their quality world. This picture was more important than the possibility of facing future abuse. As a result CPS could not return the girls to their home to live with the mother. This resulted in a decision to recant the reported abuse. Both girls then reported to CPS that their mom was right and they lied out of anger at their father.

Section 4.03 Power

An aspect of power is the need to feel inner control over one's life. When people perceive they are overly regulated from the outside, they will frequently rebel through antisocial behavior, apathy, or other negative symptoms (Wubbolding, 2000). When abuse occurs, children may experience feelings of worthlessness and anxiety that interfere with their ability to concentrate on academic work or other areas that previously provided them with effective ways of meeting their power need. The result of choosing to give up on academics, positive peer relationships, and extracurricular activities only adds to their feelings of powerlessness. Because there is the need for power, child sexual abuse victims may attempt to meet it by choosing self-defeating behaviors such as shoplifting, arson, gang activities, and sexual acting out. Erwin (2004), distinguishes between power over, power within, and power with:

1. *Power over:* exercising one's influence over something or someone.
2. *Power within:* includes learning, achieving success, and enjoying the feeling of self-worth that comes with personal growth.
3. *Power with:* Is achieved when working cooperatively with others. It is the place where the need to belong and power intersect.

In therapeutic work with sexual abuse victims, power is an issue that frequently comes up. Typically, children and their caretakers want to know:

- Why did the offender behave the way they did? (Power over)
- Will I ever feel better about myself since this happened to me? (Power within)
- Will I be able to trust or develop loving relationships? (Power with)

Clients also want to know:

- How can a sex offender be identified before he acts?
- What is the motivation behind the offender's behavior?
- Why do they choose children?

Education for parents and caretakers regarding categories of sex offenders can be useful in addressing these questions:

Article V. Male Sex Offenders: Typologies

Male sex offenders usually fall within three categories. Nicholas Groth (2001) identified two categories: fixated/pedophile and regress/situational child molester. An additional category of organic dysfunctional offenders has been added in this book.

Section 5.01 Fixated/Pedophile

1. Offender has a primary sexual attraction for prepubescent children.
2. Offenses tend to be planned, not impulsive.
3. Sexual behaviors usually involve fondling, masturbation, and nonpenetrating behaviors.
4. Emphasis of sexual arousal is on both victim and offender.
5. Fixated offenders usually perpetrate the abuse without alcohol or mood-altering drugs.

Section 5.02 Regressed/Situational Child Molester

1. Offender has a primary sexual attraction for adults.
2. Offender acts out sexually with children to cope with depression, stress, and situational life stressors.
3. Sexual behaviors vary from voyeurism to intercourse.
4. Offender's attention is primarily on his own arousal and release.
5. Regressed offenders are more likely to use alcohol or mood-altering drugs during their offenses.

Section 5.03 Organic Dysfunctional

These offenders have difficulty establishing limits on their own behavior as a result of genetic abnormalities, brain-damaging accidents, or disease related organic damage. Because of this, they sometimes choose children to meet their natural sexual impulses.

Minimal research is available on female offenders, possibly due to under-reporting and lack of public awareness. However, as a result of increased media emphasis on cases of female offenders, society is taking more interest in this area. A typology of sexual offenders has been developed that differentiates female sex offenders from male sex offenders (Matthews, Matthews, & Speltz, 1991).

Article VI. Female Sex Offenders: Typologies

There are three basic types of female sex offender.

Section 6.01 Teacher/Lover

1. Victims are typically male adolescents.
2. Offender uses role of position/power over victim.
3. Offender views behavior as an act of kindness and believes the victim was not harmed and actually enjoyed the abuse.
4. Offender doesn't view the behavior as criminal.
5. Offender usually has history of extrafamilial sexual abuse and grew up in an environment of verbal and emotional abuse.

Section 6.02 Male Coerced/Male Accompanied

1. Female offender is influenced by a male partner to engage in the sexual abuse.
2. Victim is often female and is the daughter or has a familial type relationship with the adult female.
3. Female offender takes the position of subordinate with the male offender or feels powerless and fearful of the male offender.
4. Male-coerced offenders are often reluctant to participate but fear negative consequences from the male offender.
5. Male-accompanied offenders are more self-motivated and participate more actively in the abuse.

The male-accompanied female offender was dropped from the female offender typology by Matthews et al. (1989), however more recent research (Syed & Williams, 1996) indicates this group warrants reinclusion.

r Place

OGRESS NOTE

DATE:

SESSION LENGTH			
EXPRESSIVE ART	SOLUTION-FOCUSED		
ROLE PLAY	NARRATIVE	OTHER	
GAL	ASAC	OTHER	

Section 6.03 Predisposed

1. Offender usually abuses her own children.
2. Victims are often 6 years old or younger.
3. Offender was typically abused at an early age for a number of years.
4. Predisposed offenders are more likely to have sadistic fantasies triggered by anger and to cause pain or physical harm to their victims than either teacher/lover or male-coerced/male-accompanied offenders.

Article VII. Freedom

Freedom involves having choices, and these involve our ability to choose what we say, do, and think. It also includes the desire to have a choice in what others say or do to us. Choice theory concepts teach that people cannot control anyone's behavior but their own. However, people do have choices about how they process and behave in response to other people's actions. Teens who were sexually abused prior to ever having sexual intercourse with someone of their choosing often identify anger over not being allowed to choose with whom they lost their virginity. These teens often report feeling distraught that they are now "used goods" and no longer virgins. The picture of virginity they previously held is out of balance with the fact that someone had "taken" it. Teens can benefit from examining their definition of virginity and what it means to "give it away," and exploring the emotional and physical aspects of losing virginity. The result of this process is often the conclusion that, emotionally, virginity cannot be taken from anyone until they choose to give it to the person of their choice. Acceptance can then be made that while they were controlled physically, no one can control their thoughts. This often increases both their fulfillment of freedom and power needs.

The perception of freedom can also be affected by other choices made for them as a result of their status as minors. After a disclosure of abuse, many decisions are made by social service agencies that are not desired by children or their caretakers. These include: removal from their home, placement in foster care or group homes, a change in their school district, or being asked to tell the abuse story repeatedly to CPS workers, prosecutors, and therapists with whom they have no relationship or connection.

Article VIII. Fun

Human beings have a need for fun or happiness-inducing activities. Fun includes laughing, discovering new things, learning, and the simple joys of life. Children usually do not need to be told to have fun or how to meet their need for fun. For proof, just watch children on a school playground. On the other hand, children who are experiencing and attempting to cope with abuse may have difficulty experiencing fun because of intrusive thoughts.

- Will the abuse happen again?
- When will the abuse happen again?
- What can I do to prevent the abuse from happening?
- Should I tell someone what is happening?
- What will happen to me/my family/the offender if I tell?

After children disclose, there can be additional energy-consuming thoughts.

- Will I be taken away from my family?
- When will I see my family again?
- What will people say/think if they find out I was abused?
- Will there be enough money if dad has to go to jail?
- Will my offender retaliate?

These intrusive thoughts often drain children of the energy or desire to interact and be playful. This lack of fun-seeking behaviors may also affect their peer relationships (love and belonging) and feelings of self-worth (power).

Article IX. Summary

Child sexual abuse is a worldwide problem that crosses all genders, ethnic groups, and socioeconomic boundaries. All sexual abuse results in victimization. Numerous factors, including the duration of the abuse, closeness to the offender, absence of support, disbelief, force and aggression, pleasure experienced during the abuse, and other negative life factors all help a therapist assess the level of trauma children may be experiencing. Children engage in a wide range of behaviors in the aftermath of sexual abuse. These behaviors are the child's attempt to survive, create healthy relationships, overcome feelings of powerlessness, increase freedom and enjoy their lives despite this crime against them. The emphasis will now switch to direct treatment issues and strategies with these children within each basic need.

CHAPTER 3

Survival and Self-Preservation

Courage is fear holding on a minute longer.

George S. Patton

He conquers who endures.

Persius

It is human nature to respond to perceived threats by choosing behaviors to protect survival. People attempt to obtain security, comfort, safety, and protection. Survival is also met by obtaining sufficient quantities of basic resources that include food, water, and shelter, and the maintenance of a comfortable body temperature. For the most part people meet their need for survival with few concerns except the choices available to meet this need. Some circumstances though, such as sexual abuse, may result in children perceiving that their survival is at risk. This can occur due to physical pain experienced during the sexual abuse, threats made by the abuser, and individual perceptions of what is occurring. Children are then confronted with the task of choosing behaviors and thinking processes with which to cope. Coping mechanisms are influenced by cognitive functioning levels, learned and observed behaviors, and available resources. Some coping behaviors, such as self-injury, sexual compulsivity, and suicide, can even conflict with children's ability to survive.

Article I. Self-Injury

Self-injury is commonly referred to as self-harm, self-mutilation, self-abuse, and self-inflicted violence. It is defined as deliberate self-harm without the intent to commit suicide. Self-injury is not intended to kill, but rather to relieve the unbearable emotional pain that sexual abuse survivors regard, paradoxically, as a form of self-preservation (Herman, 1997). It is therefore utilized as a coping mechanism that helps children respond to sexual abuse.

For many people the thought of someone harming themselves to feel better seems illogical. Children may discover that banging their heads, hitting, cutting, or burning themselves, pulling out their hair (trichotillomania), or painful insertion of objects into their bodies, releases tensions. Self-injury produces an intense emotional release that becomes a repetitive behavior for children because the relief is only temporary. It produces an identifiable physical source of pain that distracts from the emotional pain children experience as a part of sexual abuse. Self-injury is also performed as self-punishment that results from shame, self-blame, and guilt that often develops when children are sexually abused. Sexual abuse victims often believe they are to blame for the abuse. Children, despite the differences in size and power between them and an adult, may believe they are at fault for the abuse and that they should have been able to do something to stop the abuser. In some circumstances the offender or others directly and indirectly blame children for the abuse. Direct statements include, "You were asking for it," and "I can tell you want this because your body likes it." Indirect blaming involves observations such as, "You always dressed too sexy," and "It wouldn't have continued if you had just told someone." Children may also blame themselves because they wanted and enjoyed the nonsexual attention, gifts, money, and special privileges provided by the offender.

Sandy, age 8, described shame and self-blame for accepting money from her abusive uncle. She stated he would ask her to play a game where they flipped coins and she received the coin if she correctly guessed heads or tails. She reported he fondled her genitals and required her to sit in his lap while the game was played. She said that she always received money, which she really wanted, and therefore she blamed herself for the abuse.

It is not unusual for abusers to manipulate children into silence by providing them with money or objects that children naturally want. This helps to maintain children's silence about the abuse because they do not want the desirable gifts to be discontinued. Children do not recognize the manipulation of the situation and believe that they could have stopped the abuse if they did not accept the items. Children are also manipulated through special attention they receive from the abuser. Love and belonging is offered to children in exchange for silence. For this reason, sex offenders often seek out children who appear emotionally needy or neglected. Children want and deserve the nonsexual attention they receive but believe that the only way to maintain the relationship is to suffer the abuse. This combination of factors often results in children thinking that sexual abuse is their fault. This belief also increases the shame they experience.

In seeking to control our behavior and to shape the world around us to match our inner world or quality world, we seek to gain perceptions (Wubbolding, 2000.) Self-injury increases children's perceptions that they are in control. Children attempt to regain control over the events in their lives through the coping behaviors they choose with which to respond to sexual abuse. In these circumstances children, who assume that they have little control over the abusive behavior, will attempt to find coping behaviors to decrease their anxiety, fear, and confusion. Self-injury can increase children's beliefs that they have control. When children experience a reduction in emotional pain through self-injury they perceive the behavior as helpful. Some children view the self-care that they must give to themselves after the injurious behavior as a source of nurturing and additional control over their situation. In addition children often feel empowered or cared for because the attention they receive following the self-injury is desirable. Counseling, using a reality therapy approach, will involve having children evaluate their behavior and develop a plan to reduce their emotional pain through choices that do not include physical pain or conflict with their survival. It is also important to remember that it must be a child's decision to want to stop self-injury. If therapists or caretakers are viewed as demanding or manipulative in their attempts to decrease these behaviors children may experience even more shame or guilt. The perception that they are being judged can also increase the secrecy of the self-injury and damage the relationship with support people.

Article II. Psychological Triggers

One technique effective in reducing self-injury behaviors involves identifying psychological triggers that precede self-injury and teaching children how to reduce the emotional response to these stressors without harming themselves. It also involves helping children identify feelings and intrusive thoughts that they are attempting to control with the self-injury. Psychological triggers include situations, thoughts, and feelings that are connected to the sexual abuse. They involve sights, sounds, smells, and tastes. Other common triggers identified by child victims include people who have similar physical traits as their abuser, anniversaries of the abuse, holidays that occurred while the abuse was happening, and hearing stories of sexual abuse in the media or from some other source. In many situations children are unaware of the triggering event, yet they experience the anxiety, panic, fear, and tension they are attempting to reduce with the self-injury.

Justina, age 10, experienced sexual abuse by a male babysitter. Her mother reported that Justina had begun to scratch herself to the point where she bled and was pulling her hair out in anxiety reactions. The mother said that some of the scratches were deep and had resulted in infection. The mother could not identify any triggers or pattern of situations that preceded the self-injury. On two occasions Justina was observed in the therapist's office scratching her arms and appeared to be experiencing high levels of anxiety that she could not identify a trigger for. The mother also identified that the scratching and hair pulling had been observed at the movies, at school, and at home. A connection between the self-injury events and the sexual abuse was made by Justina during her third session when she explored possible sight, sound, smell, and taste triggers. She recalled that her abuser would make popcorn before showing her pornography and having her perform oral sex on him. For Justina, the smell of popcorn triggered emotions that were connected to the abuse situation. She had attempted to reduce these emotional states through her painful scratching and hair pulling. Through the process of identification and relaxation techniques Justina was able to eliminate her self-injury behaviors and resume activities where the smell of popcorn existed.

Triggers are sometimes difficult to identify. However, relaxation and stress reduction techniques can still provide an effective behavioral choice to coping with the anxiety and emotional pain children previously used self-injury to reduce. Self-injury behaviors are often a source of shame for the sexual abuse survivor and this shame can intensify the behavior. Relaxation techniques can be taught and practiced within the counseling session. Children can then perform these when they become aware of physiological reactions that result in the desire to perform self-injury behaviors. These reactions experienced by the child can include trembling, a racing heart, nausea, and tightening of the throat.

There are many different types of relaxation techniques. The following are stress reduction exercises that can be taught and structured in a way so that children can easily learn them and put them into practice.

Section 2.01 Self-Hypnosis

This technique involves directing oneself into a state of relaxation and suggestibility. The person, prior to beginning the process, identifies short verbal phrases (I am OK, I am a good person, I am valuable, and do not need to hurt myself, I am calming down) that can be used during the procedure. The basic steps of self-hypnosis are as follows:

1. Attempt to locate a comfortable place, where the person can sit, stand, or lie down and be free of distractions. As this technique is practiced, it will become easier to achieve the relaxed state in most environments.
2. Begin to relax by breathing deeply through the nose and slowly exhaling through the mouth while at the same time tensing and relaxing the muscles throughout the body.
3. Focus on and repeat the verbal phrases chosen.
4. Continue this process until the urge to self-harm is reduced and relaxation is obtained.

Section 2.02 Deep Breathing Exercise

Difficulty breathing or catching their breath is often described by children when they experience triggers and anxiety. This process involves the following instructions.

1. Take a long deep breath and concentrate on the air going into the body.
2. Hold the breath as long as possible and slowly release while focusing on the air leaving the body.
3. Continue the processes until normal breathing patterns are obtained.

The purpose of this exercise is twofold. First, it makes children perceive that they are back in control of the situation. Second, it reduces the runaway breathing patterns that can contribute to panic or anxiety.

Section 2.03 Progressive Muscle Relaxation

1. Find a comfortable position.
2. Beginning with the toes, tense the muscles for a count of 10, and then relax. Pay attention to the release of tension.
3. Move slowly up through the body (feet, legs, stomach, back, chest, hands, arms, neck, and face) contracting and relaxing the muscle groups.
4. Remember to breathe slowly and deeply while enjoying the body sensations of reduced tension and allowing unpleasant and intrusive thoughts to melt away as the muscles relax.

Section 2.04 Cognitive Focusing

These are mind-body techniques that reduce stress and anxiety. Their purpose is to increase relaxation

1. Clear the mind. When distracting or negative thoughts/images occur, give a *simple* command to stop them: "Go away"; "I'm in control"; or whatever is decided beforehand.
2. Imagine a peaceful scene. Concentrate on sights, smells, sounds, and tactile sensations. Some people refer to this as their safe place. If the above does not work on occasion, try focusing on a boring or repetitive mental activity (ABC song, repeating the names of classmates or cartoon characters).

An additional cognitive refocusing strategy is to repeat positive affirmations such as "I'm going to be OK"; "This will pass"; or "I am handling this." These techniques can be performed in most settings in order to calm children and provide a nonharmful choice to dealing with difficult and painful thoughts or feelings. There are many other sources therapists have reported as being helpful in reducing stress, anxiety, and the effects of triggering events. These include but are not limited to:

- Exercise
- Massage
- Yoga or martial arts
- Deep hypnosis in a therapeutic setting
- Prayer
- Aromatherapy
- Journaling
- Drawing

In addition, helping children who self-injure to learn to accept and respect their bodies is an important part of the counseling process. Providing information about physical responses to touch and accepting their body's normal functions can reduce stress when children have experienced pleasurable arousal during abuse.

Article III. Sexual Compulsivity

Sexual abuse disrupts normal sexual development (see chapter 7) and can result in the child choosing sexual behaviors to meet the needs for love and belonging, power, freedom, and fun. These behaviors in many circumstances are dangerous, result in revictimization, harm others physically and emotionally, create difficulties medically and in relationships. Examples of compulsive sexual behaviors include compulsive masturbation, dangerous sexual practices, anonymous sex, exhibitionism, voyeurism, sexual abuse of others, and prostitution/exchange of sex for commodities. Children may also act in a sexually compulsive manner based on cognitive perceptions developed from the inability to process the sexual abuse experience. These cognitive distortions include many beliefs.

1. Sexual behavior is a positive way to meet the need for love and belonging.
2. Power is obtained by initiating sexual behaviors (as opposed to being acted on).
3. Dangerous sexual experiences result in fun and excitement that cannot be matched in their strength of arousal by other behaviors.

Children who behave sexually are vulnerable to pedophiles seeking to meet their own needs for power. These sexual behaviors alert pedophiles to children's lack of boundaries and emotional difficulties. Revictimization then often validates the child's belief system that they are only worthwhile sexually. Children often value the nonsexual attention they receive from their relationship with sex offenders. This makes disclosure of their abuse less likely and may result in intensified sexual behaviors to maintain the relationship. In many situations, offenders reward children for sexualized behavior through gifts, nonsexual affection, and praise.

As children near puberty, they usually become more interested and aware of sexual activities. In many circumstances children who have been sexually abused will have more sexual information than their peers. In some cases they discover that they feel empowered and receive increased attention by acting on this knowledge. Children experience heightened levels of arousal as they attempt to meet their psychological needs through sexual behavior. This arousal state serves as an analgesic "fix" that numbs emotional pain often experienced by sexual abuse victims. Sexual compulsiveness may persist despite efforts to reduce the behavior. In fact the behaviors may become more frequent as children experience shame or guilt for not feeling in control of their behavior. Children may frequently engage in or think about sexual behaviors to the exclusion of academics or social opportunities that do not allow for sexual encounters. These behaviors also threaten children's physical health through pregnancy, STDs, and engagement in sexual relations with physically dangerous partners. Peer relationships also suffer because other children may disapprove of or feel uncomfortable around sexualized behaviors.

The treatment objectives chosen to address sexualized and compulsive behaviors are influenced by children's ages, cognitive functioning, and behaviors being exhibited. A plan for younger children should involve close supervision and provide information about the goals of sexualized behaviors to people directly involved in children's daily activities, including childcare providers or teachers. Increase the knowledge of all parties involved regarding the purpose of the child's behavior; namely, that the child is trying to meet his or her basic needs, and tell them how to provide assistance without creating further shame and the use of the Seven Deadly Habits (see chapter 1 for a listing of the Seven Deadly Habits). This creates a supportive environment for helping children change their behaviors. Teenagers also need support systems to provide accountability, and should be directly involved in choosing the people who will have knowledge of their abuse and provide support. The process of having teens help choose their support systems increases personal power and freedom. Overall, treatment planning with children who have sexual compulsions is consistent with the same type of treatment modalities used with adults who have sexual compulsions, including individual, group, and family therapy. The primary goal will be to decrease the sexually compulsive behaviors through various objectives that should include:

1. Establishing physical and emotional boundaries of self and others.
2. Increasing understanding of healthy beliefs regarding sex, sexuality, love, and relationships.
3. Identifying triggers that precede sexually compulsive behaviors.
4. Understanding the basic needs and effective choices to meet them.
5. Increasing skills training in the areas of social skill development, problem solving, anger management, and control of impulses.

Group therapy is a powerful therapeutic intervention with sexually compulsive children. Group therapy reduces feelings of shame and isolation, and also serves as a valuable setting for children to learn new behaviors and to practice new skills. One consideration, however, is to choose group members with similar levels of compulsive behaviors and emotional/chronological development. For example, it would be inappropriate to include an 8-year-old child with compulsive masturbation behaviors and an 11-year-old child who was sexually acting out on others and engaging in intercourse. Groups must serve the purpose of providing information while not escalating the child's sexual development.

There are many techniques that can be utilized with children in group sessions. Johnson and Gill (1992) describe a technique titled "Stop the Action (Hollywood Style)." This activity can also be used in individual and family counseling.

- Everyone "freezes" when the therapist says, "stop the action." Everyone instantaneously stops whatever he or she is physically doing and stops speaking, and thinks about what is occurring.
- Another version, as the use of this technique becomes clear, is to add things to look for during the group process such as sadness, anger, guilt, victimizing behavior, sexualized behavior, empathy, or cognitive distortions. Anyone can call "stop the action."

As a part of social skills development "stop the action" can be used to identify use of the Seven Deadly Habits, processing the effects of their use on others, and how to effectively use the Seven Caring Habits.

Playing "stop the action" helps children become aware of their total behavior. It increases awareness of thoughts, feelings, and somatic responses that precede behaviors. Somatic feelings are usually strong prior to acts of compulsive behaviors. Therefore, helping the child gain understanding of this process will help decrease the behaviors. Common somatic and emotional processes that precede sexual compulsivity include:

Loneliness
Boredom
Sadness
Anger
Anxiety
Arousal
Fear

Teaching emotional states is important because children usually have a limited awareness of and ability to identify emotions other than mad, sad, and happy. One way to help children learn to identify emotional responses to situations is by creating a larger vocabulary of emotional states. This helps increase children's ability to label their feelings and choose effective behaviors to deal with situations that they previously chose to cope with through sexualized behaviors.

An effect many children experience, resulting from sexual abuse, is to become emotionally numb (dissociate) and in many cases, physically numb. This allows the children to disconnect themselves from the abusive experience while the abuse is occurring and they also use it as a means of coping following the abuse. One way children learn emotions is through associations they connect with physical sensations. An example is when children report they have a stomachache when they are emotionally stressed. Counseling with choice theory can educate children about the total behavior process and help them determine options to cope with their emotions and physiological responses. Part of learning feelings includes paying attention to body sensations. Examples of physical manifestations are a tightening in the throat, trembling, shortness of breath, tears, and tingling sensations. Children can learn to connect their physiological responses to descriptive words through discussions of feeling words. There are many useful ways to increase awareness of feeling words such as feeling faces pictures (see appendix), charades, puppets, music, and art.

Section 3.01 Charades

Have the children draw slips of paper from a bowl. Each child then acts out the feeling that is written on the slip, and others in the group guess the emotion being demonstrated. This activity can be done individually or in teams.

Section 3.02 Puppets

Provide art supplies (glue, scissors, yarn, construction paper, glitter, magazines, etc.) and small paper sacks. Encourage children to choose four different feelings and construct them using the supplies. This can be a single activity or the puppets can be used to perform a play or as aids to help children describe sensations or emotions in future groups.

Section 3.03 Art

These exercises are plentiful and only limited by the imagination. Additional feeling art worksheets are included in the appendix.

Section 3.04 Music

A favorite with teens is to encourage them to bring in music or songs that represent how they feel about themselves, their families, the abuse, and any other topic they want to address. There are numerous online services that provide lyrics to almost any song, and this allows for more in-depth discussion.

By learning to identify feelings and by increasing their awareness of feelings, children can become more aware of their compulsive behaviors, including sexualization, and they can choose to reduce emotional states.

Article IV. Suicide

The ultimate self-injurious behavior that affects survival is the attempt to take one's own life — or the actual taking of one's own life. Suicide is a total behavior that people choose when they have given up on the idea that they will ever be able to get their lives back into effective control (Glasser, 1998b). Children who are unable to satisfy quality world pictures may choose to remove the final picture — themselves. This is a serious move that counselors and parents should be concerned about, because suicide among adolescents and young adults, ages 15 to 24, ranks as the second-leading cause of death in the United States (Matsakis, 1991).

Children, unable to cope with the emotional or physical pain, feelings of isolation, or lack of support to deal effectively with the sexual abuse, may determine suicide to be the best decision with which to end their suffering. After making this decision to attempt suicide children may begin to act happier. They may seem to be coping because they have made a decision that reduces the stress, anxiety, and hopelessness they were experiencing.

The ability to predict suicide among children is difficult; however, those who commit suicide frequently display some observable signs, which, if assessed early, may allow for intervention and reduce the likelihood of the suicidal act occurring. The probability of suicidal behavior increases as the number of symptoms increase. The duration and intensity of the behaviors should also be considered in making and assessment of possible suicidal behavior.

- Direct statements, such as, "I wish I were dead."
- Indirect statements that might include, "No one would miss me," or "I won't be a problem much longer."
- Expressions of hopelessness, helplessness, or anger toward self or life.
- Loss of an important person through death, divorce, or suicide.
- Previous suicide attempts.
- Changes in sleeping or eating patterns.
- Giving away important personal possessions.
- Drug/alcohol abuse.
- Withdrawal from friends, social activities, and previously enjoyable interests.
- Self-injurious behavior.
- Risk taking/careless behavior.
- Decrease in concerns about appearance, personal hygiene, and health.
- Legal involvement.
- Relationship loss because of breakup, geographical moves, changes of school, or peer conflict.
- Personal humiliation.
- High expectations of achievement by family or self.
- A poor relationship with parents, primary caregivers, or peers.
- History of poor decision making and poor social skills.
- Death themes represented through artwork and in music choices.
- Changes in school performance/behavior such as grades, homework completion, peer relationships, skipping and decreased involvement in extracurricular activities.

Sexually abused children are at a higher risk for suicide when they progress from victimization to traumatization (see factors in chapter 2). This increases when there is a close relationship with the offender or the disclosure was met with disbelief or a lack of support. In these circumstances, children become more emotionally overwhelmed and may experience difficulty in developing any effective coping mechanisms to assist them dealing with the sexual abuse. When suicidal symptoms are observed in children or reported by others, it is important to take action and immediately address the thinking patterns and feelings. It is imperative to find out if a plan has been developed.

Article V. Misconceptions about Suicide

A wide range of misconceptions exist regarding suicidal thinking, which often results in the therapist or caretakers not doing anything until it is too late and the child has attempted or committed suicide.

Section 5.01 Talking about Suicide Encourages It

Discussing whether children are thinking about or planning a suicide opens communication and allows for discussion of feelings. This often reduces the intensity of feelings that have been previously internalized. Talking about suicide provides the counselor with an opportunity to discuss whether a plan has been developed and the availability of resources to carry out the plan.

Section 5.02 Children Who Talk about Suicide Are Only Seeking Attention

All suicidal thinking needs to be taken seriously. Children who have a history of negative attention-seeking behaviors may be dismissed as not serious. It is the therapist's ethical responsibility to directly explore with children and their caretakers any suicidal thinking expressed verbally or through behavior.

Section 5.03 There Is Nothing You Can Do If
Someone Really Wants to Commit Suicide

Most people consider suicide because they have been unable to reduce their pain through any other thinking or acting behaviors. Counseling can provide children with new resources to reduce their emotional pain, obtain support, and generate new behaviors that do not conflict with the need for survival.

Section 5.04 Suicide Is Always Preventable

Regardless of the therapist's experience, training, or diligence in working with the suicidal ideation, ultimately it is the child's choice to commit or not to commit suicide.

When a counselor becomes aware of or concerned about the possibility that a child may be suicidal, a direct approach to the situation is required.

Questions that are asked in a calm and clear approach can help determine whether a child has current suicidal thinking, a plan, the resources to carry the plan through. This provides an opportunity to develop a plan for more effective behaviors to reduce the child's pain. Wubbolding (1987) outlines a series of questions that aid in assessment of lethality in suicidal threats.

1. *Are you thinking of killing yourself?* This helps determine if the threat appears possible and establishes the type of intervention needed.
2. *Have you previously tried to kill yourself?* This question is important because past suicide attempts indicate suicide has been a part of the child's coping history and is a good predictor of whether they may attempt suicide again.
3. *Do you have a plan? How will you do it?* The lethality of threat increases with a plan having been developed and the way to proceed decided on.
4. *Do you have the means to kill yourself?* Availability of the resource to carry out the suicide increases the probability that the child can carry out the plan.
5. *Will you make a contract not to kill yourself?*

A clear, time-defined, and written commitment by the child not to commit suicide can lessen lethality. This contract should not prevent the therapist from taking further action such as hospitalization. Caretaker involvement to observe commitment to the contract outside the counseling environment is also necessary.

Article VI. Summary

Regardless of the coping mechanisms previously chosen by children to deal with sexual abuse, counselors should remember to provide a nonshaming, nonblaming, and nonjudgmental environment that encourages opportunities for children to discuss painful emotions and shameful behaviors. Therapists need to be aware of the impact of verbal and nonverbal cues they may send to children when they talk about difficult situations such as self-harm, sexual compulsiveness, and suicide. The therapist's role will also include educating other support people about how to respond to these self-injury behaviors. It is important to be aware that behaviors exhibited by children that are a threat to their survival require additional training or supervision for therapists who counsel them. Also, an awareness of negative perceptions or personal bias by therapists, regarding these types of behaviors, is also important because it can impact therapeutic effectiveness. The first priority of counselors should always be to help preserve the emotional and physical survival of children through the techniques they utilize. Developing a relationship by creating a choice theory environment will be addressed in the following chapter. Children must perceive they are in a safe and trusting environment before these physically harmful coping skills are confronted.

CHAPTER 4

Connecting and Caring

Nothing you do for children is ever wasted. They seem not to notice us, hovering, averting our eyes and they seldom offer thanks, but what we do for them is never wasted.

Garrison Keillor

Human relationships are defined as a connection between two or more individuals. Children's first relationships after birth are with their families or caretakers. Relationships are then expanded to include additional caretakers, education systems, and peers. Children who are successful at obtaining positive early relationships generally express feelings of security and happiness with their lives. When children are unable to connect and meet their need for love and belonging, emotional and physical problems may develop. Through the use of reality therapy children can learn the skills necessary to build and maintain relationships. Two components of reality therapy are (1) creating a trusting relationship, and (2) helping individuals to learn the skills needed to connect with others. One aspect of helping children learn how to meet their need for love and belonging is to focus on present relationships. Reality therapy emphasizes the here and now, not the past. It is critical not to become stuck in reliving circumstances that cannot be changed. This is especially important in the treatment of sexual abuse. Reliving painful memories and emotions does not help children move forward. The past, when addressed sparingly can be useful in drawing on strengths and resilience. Sexual abuse is difficult enough to survive once, and re-experiencing abuse by recounting it in counseling can actually traumatize some children and is not considered supportive. Many therapists ask children to tell their stories based on the assumption that talking about the details will be helpful. When coercion is used by a therapist to elicit the stories, the results are a disconnection between children and therapists. Preparation for court testimony is one exception to the rule of not discussing the abuse details. The preparation for testimony serves an entirely different purpose from discussing the abuse to relive the traumatic experience that cannot be undone. The preparation for testimony can help reduce anxiety and shame by allowing children to talk about the abuse in an environment where they feel secure prior to discussing the abuse in an open courtroom.

The continuing goal of reality therapy is to create a choice theory environment between client and therapist (Glasser, 2000 b). This involves being patient, supportive, nonjudgmental, and avoiding the Seven Deadly Habits (criticizing, blaming, complaining, nagging, threatening, punishing, and rewarding in order to control). This relationship must exist before children will be willing to engage in internal evaluation and be willing to consider new behavioral choices. In a connected therapeutic relationship children are more willing to explore cognitive distortion and beliefs about their abuse. By allowing the therapist into their quality world, children have the trust necessary to take steps toward developing productive thinking and behavioral skills.

Sexually abused children's trust has been violated by abuse, and as a result building a therapeutic relationship can sometimes be a challenge. Children may exhibit a variety of behaviors toward therapists because they enter both therapy and the introduction to therapists with a variety of boundary lines. They may embrace their therapist, try to sit on a therapist's lap, or hide behind their caretaker. Therapy with sexual abuse victims involves teaching children healthy boundaries with their own as well as other people's bodies. Other children frequently shun children who have weak boundaries. Adults may also feel awkward or uncomfortable around children whose behavior involves frequent touching or appears sexualized. Indeed, sexualized behaviors can also result in children being revictimized by another sex offender when these weak boundaries are identified. An important part of the counseling process is to teach children about healthy personal space for themselves and others. This can be accomplished through stories, games, videos and discussions between children and therapists. These sessions may also involve nonoffending family members or caretakers. Some suggested resources include:

- *Let's Talk About Touching; A Therapeutic Game* (Johnson, 1992)
- *Kids Have Rights Too!* (Lennett, (1985)

- *Sometimes It's OK to Tell Secrets* (Bahr, 1988)
- *I Like You to Make Jokes with Me, But I Don't Want You to Touch Me* (Bass, 1993)
- *It's My Body* (Freeman, 1984)
- *Loving Touches* (Freeman & Deach, 1985)
- *A Better Safe than Sorry Book* (Gordon, Gordon, & Cohen, 1992)

Exploring boundaries with children helps empower them to know that they have rights and that their bodies are their own. Children also learn that they can meet their need for love and belonging without violating other people's personal space or thinking they have to act sexualized to receive love and feel a sense of belonging.

Article I. Therapist–Child Relationship

As previously noted, even at the first session, children may immediately want to hug or sit on the therapist's lap before establishing a relationship. A direct yet gentle technique is necessary to begin teaching boundaries. A suggested approach to this type of encounter is to:

1. Gently remove oneself from the physical encounter.
2. Kneel so one is at the child's eye level.
3. Smile and warmly state, "Hi, it is nice to meet you. Would you mind if we only shake hands since we have just met?"

This approach helps prevent children from thinking they have been rejected. The use of the attendant behaviors of making eye contact and getting down to the children's level demonstrates interest in them. It also begins the first steps toward teaching healthy boundaries. This process can continue upon entering the therapy office by encouraging children to choose a place to sit. Therapists can then choose a place approximately one to two arm lengths away. If children are displaying weak boundaries, therapists can introduce the concept of "Safe Space." Therapists can explain that they are going to ask some questions during the counseling session to help the child understand a safe environment. Some possible questions include:

1. When I say the words *safe space* what does that mean to you?
2. Are there any things about my office or myself that make you think you are not safe or that make you feel uncomfortable?
3. What questions do you have about what we will be doing during our sessions?
4. Are there any things that you do not want me, as your therapist, to do?

5. What ideas do you have about what you would like to do during your sessions?
6. Do you know what brought you here?

Based on these questions children can begin to understand that they have choices in therapy. For many children this may be the first time that someone has asked them, "What do you want?" This is empowering. Reality therapy encourages therapists to do the unexpected. With children, the unexpected can be as simple as being interested in their ideas, allowing them to establish boundaries, and giving them choices.

Another treatment intervention that children often enjoy is "Body Drawing." It is important to discuss this intervention with children first and ask their permission to do it. Proceed only when children consent and seem comfortable.

1. Begin by having the child lie on a piece of paper the size of their body from head to toe.
2. Outline the child's body with a crayon or marker.
3. Ask the child to choose colors that represent different statements such "no touch," "OK to touch," or similar statements, and color the picture.

In conjunction with this exercise, therapists can help children identify statements that they can use when someone touches a "no touch" area or anything else that results in a perception that their safe space is being invaded. A sentence completion exercise can be helpful in this process.

1. It's OK for you to_____.
2. I don't like it when you_____.
3. I would rather_____.
4. When you_____I feel_____.

Children who have been sexually abused are at higher risk for revictimization. Therefore it is important to prepare children as to how they can disclose any future abuse. A writing/drawing exercise that can be used for this is the "Quality World Safety Plan."

1. Children are asked to write inside the heart the names of all the people they could tell if someone abused them.
2. Children are then asked to evaluate whether each person is capable of helping. For example, a teacher or counselor is legally obligated to help, whereas an 8-year-old friend is not.
3. Children then develop a plan or identify statements to clearly identify what occurred, such as, "(person) touched me (where) and I

Fig. 4.1 Quality world safety plan.

want you to help me make them stop." Children are encouraged to tell as many people possible until the abusive behavior stops.

4. Ask children for a commitment to the plan.

This type of exercise meets the criteria for an effective reality therapy plan in that it is simple, repetitive, realistic, controlled, and committed to by children. The therapist should also keep in mind that these techniques would not be effective unless children perceive their therapists as genuine and trustworthy.

Article II. Court Advocacy

When providing treatment for sexual abuse it is not uncommon for referred children to be expected to testify in court. The therapist can aid children and caretakers in preparing for the rigors of the process. There may be fear about the trial and providing testimony. This may result from concerns about retaliation from the offender or the offender's friends or family. Offenders often attempt to keep children from disclosing by threatening to harm them or people they care about. Children may also experience shame and concern about testifying to events of the abuse in front of the jury, offender, and other people in the courtroom. Often, the most difficult aspect of testifying for children is the realization that their testimony may result in someone they care about going to prison. It is important to remember that the people in the children's quality world are not easily removed. Children's goal in disclosure is usually to stop the abuse while at the same time not wanting anything else to change in their lives. Children often have a black-and-white, all-or-nothing view of situations. The therapist's role is to help them understand that they can still love the offender and dislike the way the offender behaved to them.

The therapist's role in preparing children and caretakers involves several components:

1. Education about the legal process.
2. Identify fears and distorted beliefs.
3. Empowerment and preparation for testimony.
4. Establish connected relationships between the family, collaborative agencies, and the legal system.
5. Familiarization with the courtroom and proceedings.
6. Identification of support systems that will be available during the trial.
7. Debriefing following the trial.

The case of Laura and Lana presented in chapter 2 attests to the power of a strong therapeutic relationship and how it supports children.

Laura and Lana refused to testify against their father out of fear of retaliation by him and his family members who had threatened them after the disclosure. The girls initially had minimal support systems (including their mother), and felt they were alone in having been sexually abused. The therapist had the girls participate in a teen sexual abuse group with other females who had already testified or were about to testify. Both girls began to report feeling less alone in the abuse and started to choose positive relationship-connecting behaviors both within the group and at school. Both were soon requesting the opportunity to confront their mother about her disbelief. Due to their interactions and information gained in individual and group settings, both girls were able to testify. The father was found guilty and received a sentence that would not make him eligible for parole until the girls were young adults.

Article III. Therapist–Caretaker Relationship

Parents and caretakers who are helping children heal from sexual abuse are also experiencing a life crisis. They too may be dealing with their own denial, anger, self-blame, and fear of the changes occurring in their lives. Families may experience negative reactions or lack of support from extended family, friends, neighbors, and coworkers. These behaviors result in the family's increased isolation. Even well-meaning people may make remarks that minimize or rationalize the abuse. These types of statements include, "I bet you are glad there wasn't rape involved," or "He only did it because he was drinking, drugging, or unhappy." Others may make more blaming statements to the nonoffending family members such as, "How could you not know that was going on?" or "I'm glad I don't put my kids in daycare." Families who identify the home as unsafe or express concerns about victimized children becoming sexual abusers may shun the family. Caretakers need a supportive environment in which to process their thoughts, feelings, and behaviors. A caretakers' support group for non-offending caretakers can meet the needs for belonging, power, freedom, and even fun. The group serves an educational purpose of providing information about the effects of sexual abuse, coping behaviors, normal sexual development, sex offender traits, and court testimony.

Katy, 35, was referred after her daughters disclosed sexual abuse by their father. Katy stated she did not believe the abuse occurred. She identified the behavioral problems her daughters were exhibiting and believed that lying was just another of their problems. A brief summary of Katy's life included being raised by alcoholic parents, sexual abuse by a brother, becoming pregnant at 17, quitting school, and marrying the child's father. She described her husband as physically abusive and controlling in that she was cut off from contact with her family and friends. Katy had never held a job in 18 years and did not have her GED. She felt she needed her husband to stay in the home due to his financial support of the family. The therapist chose to focus on establishing a relationship with Katy and not challenging her disbelief. The therapist also recommended that she attend the caretakers' support group in order to meet others who were in similar circumstances. Through her contact with other parents, Katy realized her daughters' negative behaviors were poor choices they had been using in order to cope with the abuse by their father. Katy identified her fear of not being able to take care of her family financially by herself. Katy was referred to a local agency that helped her obtain her GED and set up vocational training. She temporarily signed up for public assistance to keep her home and take care of the children's survival needs. She began therapy with her children and provided support to them during the trial proceedings. The relationships she gained through therapy and her support group empowered her to re-establish contact with her own parents and siblings, which over time became stronger. The children were returned to her care after the father's incarceration.

Therapists will be most effective when they offer clients a warm and nonjudgmental environment. Clients, who may be initially distrustful or have a limited history of connected relationships, will not be willing to evaluate their own behaviors unless they perceive the therapist as genuine and caring. Clients benefit most when they understand the therapist's approach to treatment, therefore teaching choice theory is an important part of the counseling process. By understanding reality therapy and choice theory concepts, clients are more likely to become trusting within the therapist–caretaker relationship.

Article IV. Parent–Child Relationship

A strong relationship that involves attachment and trust with a parent or caretaker can increase the chances of children disclosing sexual abuse and healing with the least amount of trauma possible. However, when children are responded to with disbelief or lack of protection the possibility of psychological trauma increases and it is likely that there will be increased disconnection in the parent/caretaker–child relationship. Reconnecting this relationship can be difficult because of legal involvement or the lack of desire by the parents or children. When the circumstances do allow for contact between parents and their children it is therapeutically ideal to begin individual sessions with each party discussing the structure of contact and individual issues at that time. Children in these circumstances often reside outside the parental home and will be experiencing numerous changes and stressors that include thoughts about the abuse, lack of belief by important caregivers/family members, changes in school, foster/residential placement, and limited contact with family. Although these changes are often necessary to provide safety for children, it is important to address these areas of loss that may have provided some of the strength to cope with the pressure, prior to disclosure. These losses include pets, friends, teachers, and extracurricular activities and leaders.

As previously discussed, children do not necessarily remove a nonsupportive parent from their quality world but may modify their picture of this parent. Children may want contact with their nonoffending parent and, in cases of incest, their offender. In some circumstances this type of contact can occur even prior to the completion of legal proceedings and be in children's best psychological interest. Therapeutic visitation can provide the opportunity for this when certain parameters can be established and agreed upon by all parties (parent, social service agency, courts, therapist, and child) involved in the case. These criteria include:

- The child requests contact.
- The parent does not discuss court proceedings or the sexual abuse.
- The parent is not considered violent or emotionally unstable.
- The parent is observed during contacts to be positive toward the child, both verbally and nonverbally.

When appropriate, this type of contact can reduce stress for children who want and need contact with family members. Many children report thinking they are being punished for the disclosure because of the loss of contact between them and their families. These sessions may also reduce the possibility of children recanting abuse based on their belief that recanting will return them to their family. Following legal completion of sexual abuse cases, some children ask to confront nonsupportive or disbelieving parents. A well-planned therapy session can provide this opportunity. Children should first be helped to examine what they hope to obtain from a confrontation and be realistic about possible outcomes. Without awareness and the ability to accept that they may continue to be reacted to with disbelief, children may actually be further psychologically traumatized. However, when a confrontation is approached with the understanding that it will provide an opportunity for children to express thoughts and feelings about the effects of the abuse and disbelief, children can emerge with feelings of empowerment. Another way to approach a confrontation without face-to-face contact is to assist children in writing a letter to those they want to confront. This can result in the same positive outcomes when children do not want contact or contact is not possible

Letter writing can also be a useful tool to help children clarify their thoughts before a confrontation or to use in the therapy setting utilizing the Gestalt empty chair technique. In the empty chair technique children are asked to envision that the person they want to confront is sitting in a chair in front of them. Some children may choose to put a picture of the person, an object, or drawing in the chair. Children can then choose to read a prepared letter or say whatever they want to the "person" without fear of retaliation. This technique can be very powerful, and a "cooling off" period immediately following it should be scheduled to include relaxation exercises and de-escalation of emotions.

Article V. Attachment Disruptions

Caretakers and children can experience great difficulties when attachment does not occur. Disruptions in attachment, which generally occur in the first 3 years of a child's life, can result in psychological issues that cause children to have problems with trust and forming attachments in later life.

Children are at a higher risk for attachment disruptions when any of the following are experienced between birth and the age of 3.

- Sudden abandonment or separation from the mother. This can result from the death or incarceration of the mother, or adoption or foster home placement of the child.
- Sexual, physical, or emotional abuse or neglect.

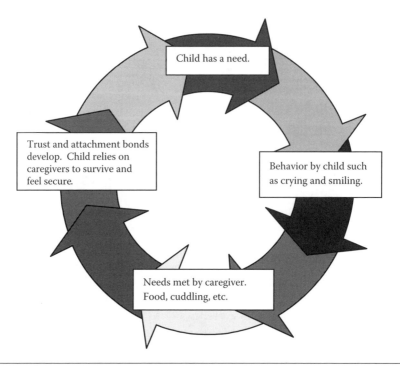

Fig. 4.2 Needs-satisfying attachment cycle.

- Depression or other mental disorders exhibited by the mother.
- Mothers who are self-centered, who have poor parenting skills, and have poor parenting responses.
- Multiple foster placements or failed adoptions.
- Undiagnosed or painful illness such as ear infections, colic, or surgeries.
- Drug or alcohol abuse by the mother during pregnancy.

Even past the age of 3, children who have had some attachment or bonding abilities can experience difficulties if the previous problems have been severe. Children who experience attachment difficulties have a wide range of behaviors that cause frustration for both the caretakers and their children.

Children who experience these behaviors are frequently diagnosed with reactive attachment disorder (RAD), oppositional defiant, attention-deficit disorder, and bipolar disorder. Regardless of the label placed on these children, the results of poor attachments cause difficulties with the ability of these children to form close attachments. The children can grow up with sociopathic behaviors, which are a result of having no conscience. They have many beliefs, which need to

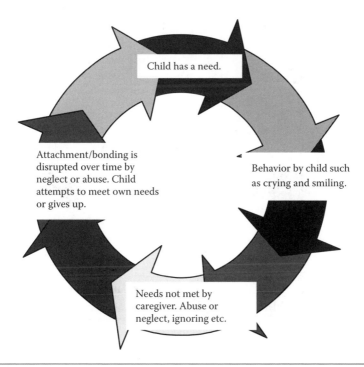

Fig. 4.3 Disrupted attachment cycle.

be addressed in treatment, such as "Loving hurts" and "Why should I care. People will just get rid of me or hurt me anyway." Children with attachment difficulties do not trust parenting so they choose to parent themselves and attempt to meet their basic needs any way they can. They can appear bright, loving, attractive, hopeless, lost, independent, and charming in order to manipulate others. They are willing to lie, steal, and horde food or other items. Because they do not trust adults, they are constantly trying to assess other people's motives and the "next move." It is important to recognize that these behaviors have served a valuable purpose — physical or emotional survival.

Many sexually abused children develop attachment disruptions from being exposed to other forms of abuse and neglect in their homes. This ability to bond with or trust others can be further damaged by multiple foster placements, by repeated victimizations, or emotionally unavailable adult caregivers. The behaviors of these children (see Figure 4.3) are the consequences of numerous placements in foster homes, with other relatives, or in youth care centers, all of which further exacerbates their attachment problems.

Table 4.1 Behaviors in Attachment-Disrupted Children

Infants	Preschoolers and older children
Resist cuddling and affection	Oppositional and defiant behaviors
Lack of reciprocal smiling	Poor peer relationships
Fear, withdrawal, rage, excessive whining	Superficially charming and manipulative
Poor eye contact	Affectionate only on their terms
Lack of tracking	Avoid eye contact
Avoid other children	Lack of conscience or empathy
Delayed crawling, walking, or speech	Controlling, sneaky, and bossy
Indifference to people	Preoccupation with sex, violence, blood
Defensive or flinching behaviors	High-risk behaviors such as stealing or firesetting
Poor sucking response or lethargy	Abusive to other children and animals

Intervention with attachment-disrupted children is most effective in the first 3 to 4 years of life. Adult caregivers must be highly committed to helping these children and must understand (1) how the disruptions occurred; (2) what behaviors they can do to help; and (3) what behaviors can be harmful and cause more detachment.

Article VI. Attachment-Building Behaviors: Infants to Age 3

- *Eye contact:* Always make warm, happy, and approving eye contact when speaking to a child.
- *Smiling:* The child must see it in your eyes.
- *Touch:* Sling wearing to carry an infant is highly recommended.
- *Repeat:* Redo earlier developmental stages the child may have missed.
- *Bottles:* Caretakers should always hold bottles during feedings. Do not prop the bottle up.
- *Voice:* Tone should always be soft, soothing, and lighthearted.
- *Activities:* Read, sing, or recite nursery rhymes to the child.
- *Sleeping behaviors:* Cosleep or allow the child to sleep next to the caregiver's bed whenever possible.
- *Out of the primary home caregiving:* Use only in emergencies.

When children are identified as having attachment problems in preschool or as older children, additional caregiver behaviors are needed. Children in this age group will display more aggressive and defiant behaviors that require more patience and commitment by the caregivers than with younger children.

Article VII. Attachment-Building Behaviors:
Preschoolers and Older Children

- Be clear and firm with expectations and consequences. Attachment-disrupted children will not respect adults whom they believe they can control and manipulate.
- Use the Seven Caring Habits. Avoid the Seven Deadly Habits when communicating (see chapter 1).
- Praise positive behaviors. Do not overdo this or it will be perceived as manipulation.
- Encourage time-out and self-evaluation for the child and caregivers (see Self-Evaluation Questions in chapter 1).
- Use respite only for emergencies in the first year of forming attachment.
- Use and request eye contact during conversations.
- Establish and closely monitor play dates and peer socializations.
- Monitor interactions with family pets.
- Don't double up on school punishments. Allow the school to establish its own consequences and keep these separate from home life.
- Engage in activities that require interaction. Such activities include board games, working on a mutual chore, gardening, auto mechanics, etc.

Attachment-disrupted children require a large amount of one-on-one interaction; therefore, these children are more likely to overcome their earlier attachment traumas when placed in single-child families or when they are the youngest child in a placement. This allows for attachment to occur without the child having to compete with other younger children who also are in need of frequent interactions with the caregivers. When these children are able to regain some ability to trust and bond with adults and caregivers, then they are ready to focus on the other important form of bonding, establishing peer relationships.

Section 7.01 Books by Sears and Sears

William Sears and Martha Sears have identified many more attachment-building behaviors in their series of books about attachment parenting, which provide additional insight into attachment and bonding behaviors with infants, young children, and caregivers.

> *The Discipline Book: How to Have a Better Behaved Child from Birth to Age Ten* (1995)
> *The Attachment Parenting Book: A Commonsense Guide to Understanding and Nurturing Your Baby* (2001)

The No-Cry Sleep Solution: Gentle Ways to Help Your Baby Sleep through the Night (2002)

The Baby Book: Everything You Need to Know About Your Baby from Birth to Age Two (2003)

It is helpful to provide parents and caretakers with education on how to stay connected or reconnect with their children. Stress, denial, and a lack of parenting skills can cause damage to relationships with their children. Through education about how to use choice theory concepts, these parents and caretakers can develop new behaviors that strengthen the adult–child relationship. It is also useful to encourage and discuss how these adults can effectively meet their own individual basic needs. This includes establishing healthy relationships with other adults.

Article VIII. Children's Social Relationships

Sexual abuse can have a profound effect on children's relationships with others. Some sexually abused children develop the belief that sexualized behavior will gain them the love and sense of belonging that they need. Sexual offenders often encourage this belief through giving attention to children when they act sexual and minimizing attention to other qualities and skills children possess. Children may be willing to accept any attention, even sexual abuse, over being ignored. Children can begin to believe they are only valued for what they can offer sexually to others and therefore act sexualized to gain attention. Teenagers may engage in promiscuous behaviors in their attempts to gain recognition. When peers respond by giving them attention for this behavior this validates the effectiveness of sexualized behavior.

During childhood sexual abuse, sexuality may become paired with fear, anger, helplessness, pain, and anxiety. Subsequent experiences of these feelings can trigger a cycle that leads to sexual arousal, reinforcing the negative pairing (Ryan, 1999). Children may react to uncomfortable emotions through sexualized behaviors such as public or private compulsive masturbation, sexually acting out on younger or emotionally vulnerable peers, or seductive behaviors. These attempts to reduce their emotional states through sexual behaviors can result in social isolation, and that in turn may increase the sexual acting out. The repetitive aspect of the behavior creates the illusion that they have power and control in their life. The treatment focus for this issue involves identification, evaluation, and plan development for effective responses to emotional states.

Beth, 13 years old, referred for sexual abuse, the offender being an uncle living in her home, identified peer relation problems as her biggest stressor. She reported being suspended from school due to a fight when she hit a schoolmate who called her a "slut" and accused her of having sex with the girl's boyfriend. Beth stated she was sexually active with several boys, some of whom did have girl friends. She reported that she felt good and that she was in control when she was able to entice boys to have sex with her. She said that her behavior with boys was resulting in a bad reputation and rejection by a *group* of girls she had previously thought of as friends.

Beth was willing to accept that her behaviors were causing her difficulty and was committed to looking at alternative ways to meet her psychological needs. A brief education in choice theory concepts and discussion, based on a worksheet, "What Do I Want?" (see appendix A for worksheet) helped Beth clarify her issues and develop a plan she believed would result in getting what she wanted.

Her peers initially met Beth's new behaviors and activities with distrust and continued rejection. Beth was committed to continuing to try to change her reputation and within 3 months she began to feel acceptance by other students in the school drama department and began spending time with these new friends outside of school. She also reported enjoying her new appearance and the fact that her grades had improved.

Sexualized behaviors in children take on many forms that can include sexual behavior with peers, animals, self-injurious masturbation, and other indicators of age-inappropriate sexual knowledge. The purpose of sexualized behaviors in children may meet several goals.

- Decreases anxiety, tension, or other uncomfortable psychological processes.

Table 4.2 What Do I Want?

1. What do I want? <u>Friends, not to be called a slut.</u>
2. What am I doing that prevents me from getting what I want? <u>Having sex with lots of boys, dressing sexy at school, fighting, smoking.</u>
3. What am I willing to do that is different? <u>Everything but quit smoking.</u>
4. What needs am I trying to meet by my current behaviors? <u>Belonging, power, freedom, fun.</u>
5. What can I do differently to meet my needs? <u>Saying hi to people and calling my old friends and apologizing for the things I did (Belonging); doing my homework/ getting better grades and trying out for the play (Power); realize I can change to get what I want (Freedom); going shopping for new clothes/makeup and going to the new rollerblade park (Fun).</u>

- Gains attention/love and belonging.
- Retaliation.
- Increases feelings of power/being in control.
- Re-experiences pleasurable feelings learned through sexual abuse.

In addition to sexual behaviors resulting in disruption of peer relationships, sexually abused children may experience difficulties in social relationships because of underdeveloped social skills. Children who do not form close or satisfying relationships often miss out on social learning experiences that lead to skill development needed to engage others socially, maintain relationships, resolve conflicts, and communicate effectively with others. Emotional consequences also develop such as low self-esteem/self-worth and emotional isolation. Numerous factors may lead to social rejection of children:

1. *Disruptive behavior:* anger, class clowning
2. *Anxious behavior:* shyness, hyperactivity, tics
3. *Physical differences:* handicaps, ethnicity, physical unattractiveness, birth defects, clothing
4. *Dysfunctional family behaviors:* alcoholism, abuse, criminal activity
5. *Poor boundaries with self/others:* bullying, sexualized behavior, nonassertiveness, theft
6. *Intellectual differences:* learning delays, gifted intelligence

Childhood social skill difficulties can have profound effects that extend into adulthood. (Hartup, 1992) reported that "the single best childhood predictor of adult adaptation is not school grades or classroom behavior, but rather, the adequacy with which a child gets along well with other children. Those who are generally disliked, are aggressive and disruptive are unable to sustain close relationships with other children and cannot establish themselves in the peer culture are at risk." Adulthood risks include poor mental health, dropping out of school, low achievement, and poor employment history (Katz & McCellan, 1997).

Children who lack adequate social skills benefit from individual and group counseling. This process works best in conjunction with a parent/caretaker education process on how to assist social development outside the counseling environment.

Article IX. Social Skills Treatment Planning

1. Individual sessions with the child:
   a. Therapist–child trust building
   b. Problem identification and evaluation

    c. Emotion/feeling identification

    d. Healthy peer relationship factors

2. Group sessions for the child:

    a. Group cohesion/trust building

    b. Games and activities that promote sharing/working together

    c. Opportunities for leadership and following directions

3. Parent education:

    a. Using the Seven Caring Habits regularly

    b. Parent–child play/activities to be performed outside therapy

    c. Family meetings/identifying problem-solving opportunities

    d. Inquiring about children's daily events/interests

    e. Encouragement and support of interests/self-esteem increasing activities

    f. Intervention/discipline and avoiding punishment

In the first phase of treatment, children learn to identify emotions in themselves/others and appropriate behavioral responses, which increases their social competence. One technique that can be used with any age group involves showing pictures of same-aged peers in various emotional states. For cost effectiveness, pictures can be cut out of magazines by the therapist or as part of an individual or group exercise. The therapist then asks:

1. What do you think this person is feeling?
2. What might have happened that resulted in someone feeling this way?
3. What could this person do to feel better?

Another technique that personalizes the experience is to request that children draw or tell a story about a situation that resulted in their feeling happy, sad, mad, or scared. More complex emotions can be offered for older groups of children. Following identification of the situation children are asked to identify their thoughts, behavioral, and body responses to the situation. This allows children to become aware of *total behavior.*

Groups provide a hands-on experience for social skill development. It allows children, in a controlled environment, to interact and observe emotional responses to both their behavior and the impact their behavior has on others. It also provides opportunities to try out new skills identified during individual sessions. Regardless of the age group, therapists may need to make children aware of specific behaviors and encourage self-evaluation. For example, with younger children, "Robert, did you notice that Jane cried when you pushed her. How do you think she may be feeling?" Following this, the group can discuss ways to handle frustration during play. The same approach can be used with adolescents, such as, "Beth, what do you think Amanda may have felt when you told her that you thought her shoes were stupid?" Then use the opportunity to discuss individual differences and that thinking something does not have to lead to verbal expression.

Article X. Summary

Sexual abuse causes harm in children's ability to trust. This is the foundation for long-term relationships. During the healing process from sexual abuse children will benefit from having many support systems that model and encourage healthy relationships. This includes the therapist–child, parent–child, and social relationships. These support systems strengthen resilience, rebuild and redefine relationships, all of which provide a strong foundation for children to heal.

CHAPTER 5

Personal Empowerment

Where there is hope, there is life; where there is life, there is possibility; and where there is possibility, change can occur.

Jesse Jackson

By definition, child sexual abuse involves the use of power and control by someone with greater status, influence, authority, and experience than the child. It involves manipulation, coercion, and occasionally physical violence. However, it is not necessary to physically harm children to have them submit to or not disclose sexual abuse. In many situations the abuser has an established relationship with the child that allows gradual violation of the child's boundaries. In these circumstances the child is unaware of the events being sexually abusive until the situation has progressed to a point where the child feels helpless or responsible for the abuse. Also, as discussed in chapter 4, the child may succumb to the abuse and be unwilling to disclose because of a wish to maintain the nonsexual aspects of the relationship, and would feel guilty and responsible if the offender were to be punished as a result of the disclosure. Direct violence is also not necessary when the child recognizes that the offender is capable of physical abuse. The child may have witnessed or be aware of the offender having been physically abusive or threatening to other people. This recognition allows for increased power over the child by the offender.

To aid in the understanding of this chapter, there are several definitions that need to be made clear.

Power: maintaining influence over the behavior, attitudes, and feelings of another. It involves verbal and nonverbal statements communicated to another person as to how they should behave and think.

Control: Maintaining a check on one's behavior, attitudes, and feelings. It involves actions and beliefs about how a person should live his or her life.

Power over: Acknowledges basic physical and cognitive differences between the abuser and child.

Power with: Incorporates the learning and achievements obtained through working cooperatively with others (discussed in chapter 4 as social skills development).

Power within: Includes aspects of internal empowerment such as self-control, self-worth, learning, and achieving success. This will also be referred to as personal power.

Counseling sexually abused children with choice theory principles focuses on increasing personal power, which is most within the child's scope of influence. Sexually abused children usually view themselves as victims and powerless over the abuse. This is correct from the standpoint that they could not control the abuser's behavior. Choice theory can help them become aware of what they *do* have control over (their actions regarding and thinking processes about the abuse). This results in children viewing themselves as survivors. In some situations children may attempt to overcome feelings of low self-worth and powerlessness by becoming aggressive. They may be labeled as bullies, sex offenders, or as having some type of impulse control disorder. Children attempt to reduce their perception of themselves as victims by overcompensating and becoming offenders. Their behaviors may be emotionally, physically, and sexually abusive to others. Counseling in these circumstances involves development of coping skills by the child that do not violate the boundaries of others. This can be achieved through the child learning skills that increase self-worth and self-control, which lead to greater personal power or power within.

Article I. Self-Worth

Children's development of self-identity is influenced by their life experiences. These experiences affect how they feel about themselves. They also influence how children act toward others. Children who have been sexually abused often develop doubts about their value as people. How others reacted to the disclosure also affects how the children view themselves. Whether a child was blamed or supported, shamed or nurtured, believed or not believed, and provided with learning resources or left to figure out their situation alone, all contribute to how a child thinks about him- or herself and chooses to cope. Sexual abuse victims have identified many negative beliefs that impact self-worth.

- The abuse was my fault.
- I am helpless.
- People will not like me if they know.
- People will think I am gay if they know.
- My body is disgusting/betrayed me.
- I must be perfect to overcome this.
- No one else has had this happen.
- I deserved this.
- What I want doesn't matter.
- I must protect my family at all cost.
- My feelings are bad/stupid/don't matter.
- Trusting people is dangerous.
- If I am unattractive I won't be abused again.
- I am dirty/broken/used.
- I feel guilty.
- Sex is bad/confusing/a way to get my needs met.

Helping identify negative beliefs and creating new thinking patterns will be a part of the treatment for the sexually abused child.

An exercise that can be used with children to assess their perceived value or self-worth is to have them identify adjectives that describe their thoughts about themselves (see appendix, "Perceived Value Adjectives"). Younger children can be read statements such as the above list of false beliefs and asked to respond "yes" or "no" (see appendix: "False Beliefs").

Another exercise is to have the child draw four perception pictures. The first picture is how they view themselves and the second, how others see them. The third and fourth pictures will be how they would like to view themselves and how they would like others to see them. This provides an opportunity to establish goals for change (see appendix, "Picture Me!").

Negative thoughts affect self-worth and hinder personal power. Counseling with the use of questions such as, "Does thinking this way help you feel better?" helps the child become aware that she has control over how she feels. This provides a transition to discussing strengths and positive attitudes the child possesses and can develop. Drawing and writing exercises appeal to all age groups and also provide choices based on personal preference or skills. The "minibook" is one set of worksheets that are combined to form a self-worth book for children (worksheets are included in the appendix).

1. *What I feel proud about:* relationships, accomplishments, objects, pets, personal attributes, skills, hobbies, sports.
2. *Things I do well:* academics, sports, hobbies, interests.
3. *How I have fun:* how the child likes to spend his or her time.
4. *What I feel happy about:* people, places, things.
5. *Things I would like to learn:* information, skills, talents.
6. *My favorite memory:* a moment that brought joy and comfort.
7. *Something I overcame:* a situation or conflict the child has experienced.
8. *Three wishes I have:* things hoped for.
9. *People who care about me:* therapist, family, caretakers, teacher.

It is empowering for children to combine these nine drawings into a minibook that can be referred back to at times when children are experiencing stress or are devaluing themselves. It is a total behavior exercise because it employs acting (looking at the book), thinking ("I can control how I feel by choosing this action"), feeling (a shift from negative to positive), and physiology (reduces anxiety and increases a calmer physiological state). It is also useful to make two to three copies of the book that can be kept in convenient places such as home, school, and the therapist's office.

One aspect of self-worth is learning and achievement. Exploring areas with children and caretakers to improve or expand learning will greatly improve self-worth in children. Responses to sexual abuse may interfere with the learning process. Children may attempt to overachieve, give up or rebel in the academic setting and when other learning opportunities present themselves.

Article II. Perfectionism

Children who cope by means of perfectionism (overcompensation) are attempting to overcome internalized messages of being worthless, stupid, and bad. These children are diligent in their studies, homework, extracurricular activities, and peer activities. When they fail to accomplish the impossible (being perfect) their negative beliefs about themselves are validated. In the therapy and school setting these children are often praised for their high achievement expectations and overlooked as having emotional difficulties because their coping behaviors appear positive. Perfectionism is not positive, however, due to it being unattainable and highly stressful to the child's emotional and physical health. Parents, therapists, and teachers often externally reward perfectionism and thereby encourage these behaviors. This may also result in the child beginning to strive to meet these external expectations and not focus on internal processes

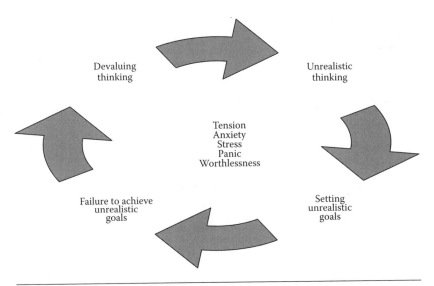

Fig. 5.1 Perfectionism cycle.

to increase self-worth. Perfectionists fear making mistakes, which they equate with being a failure and letting down those who praise them. As a result they avoid learning in new situations or attempting new experiences where they do not anticipate success. Due to this they also miss out on chances to learn and experience personal growth. Perfectionism is a cycle of unrealistic thinking and behaving coupled with negative feelings and physiological processes.

Counselors, families, and teachers need to give equal concern to both the child who is overcompensating and the child who is underachieving. Unfortunately, the child who is bringing home straight As, excelling in extracurricular activities, and is committed to other activities, is often overlooked. It is important to provide these children with the tools to develop healthy attitudes about learning, achievement, and themselves. Beginning this process includes exploring the cycle of perfectionism and identifying the thinking and behaviors that fuel the cycle. Following this step, children can begin to examine and outline their goals for change. The therapist can aid this process through supportive and direct questions.

1. How do your perfectionist behaviors conflict with what you want?
2. What beliefs are interfering with your efforts to change?
3. Which behaviors would you like to change?
4. Which beliefs do you want to let go of?
5. What would you be willing to do instead (re: 3 and 4).
6. When will you start this plan?

This process is aimed directly at the development of new thinking and acting components of total behavior. The questions may need to be modified for age-appropriate understanding. By helping children create healthy attitudes about achievement, they will be able to let go of self-defeating habits and begin to enjoy learning and healthy risk taking or trying new skills. This will also help the child learn the process of learning and not just be focused on outcomes.

Article III. Achievement Difficulties

On the other end of the continuum are the children who struggle to learn because they are overwhelmed emotionally by the sexual abuse. It may be because they are in the midst of the abuse occurring, attempting to cope alone, or they are trying to deal with other aftereffects of a disclosure about sexual abuse.

Put yourself in the child's world. Imagine for a moment that you just learned that someone you loved and trusted has betrayed and violated your trust. You are experiencing great pain and confusion. Now you must go to work and focus on a training program where you must learn a new task that will be the foundation for your future with the company. There is no one you think you can talk to about this. You are ashamed and believe you were to blame for the other person's behavior.

How do you think this personal situation may affect your ability to concentrate on learning critical new skills at the training? Is it possible you will be distracted and miss vital information? May others misjudge your reasons for being unfocused?

This is the experience of the traumatized child in the classroom. These children are often labeled as daydreamers, short attention spanned, learning and emotionally disabled, and conduct disordered. In reality they are doing the best they can to survive and these behaviors can interfere with others' needs and wants. Under these circumstances parent–teacher–therapist collaborative efforts are critical to addressing classroom and learning difficulties. This team effort can identify how to establish a positive learning environment and reduce behavioral problems. For this effort to be successful the teacher has to believe a different approach is needed and be willing to implement a new plan. It is not the role of the therapist or parent to tell a teacher how to structure their classroom. Choice theory emphasizes that you cannot change what someone else does. The teacher must want to consider new options. There are several resources available for teachers and school administrators who are open to a choice theory approach.

The School for Quality Learning (Crawford, Bodine, & Hoglund, 1993)
The Classroom of Choice (Erwin, 2004)
Schools Without Failure (Glasser, 1975)
The Quality School: Managing Students Without Coercion (Glasser, 1992)
Choice Theory in the Classroom (Glasser, 1998a)
The Quality School Teacher (Glasser, 1998c)
Every Student Can Succeed (Glasser, 2000)
Educating for Responsibility and Quality: Intervention Strategies (Hoglund, 2006)

Some common classroom problems reported by teachers regarding sexually abused children's behavior include daydreaming, anger management problems, and high motor activity. These issues all impede children's ability to learn and the latter two disrupt the classroom and learning for other children. A combined understanding of the goals of the misbehavior and how to provide positive responses will encourage a healthy outlook and development of a quality classroom environment.

Dissociative Reactions

Disassociation is mistakenly identified as daydreaming and associated with lack of interest in the classroom. A child who is dealing with emotions such as fear, confusion, and anger may cope through dissociative processes and becoming emotionally numb. This coping behavior does not come equipped with the ability to turn it on when needed (during abuse episodes) and off when it impairs other processes (learning in the classroom). Therefore dissociative behavior may occur frequently in the classroom. When this process is misunderstood a teacher may respond by using one or more of the Seven Deadly Habits: criticizing, blaming, complaining, nagging, threatening, punishing, and bribing. This response may actually increase the dissociative behaviors.

A suggested approach to dealing with this behavior in the classroom involves including the child in the changes that will occur. The teacher can begin by talking to the child and identifying an awareness of the child's difficulty in focusing on classroom tasks. Explain that some new things are going to be tried to help her come back into focus. By expressing concern about a child's learning and responses to his or her behavior, the child is less likely to feel suspicious or manipulated. This openness increases trust and the possibility of success with this technique. These behaviors by the teacher also do not result in bringing attention to the child by classmates and increasing his or her emotional discomfort.

1. Personally identifying that the child is acting dissociative.
2. Moving closer to the child.
3. Quietly speaking the child's name if moving closer did not reduce the behavior.
4. Additional verbal cues to refocus involve quietly asking, "Is everything OK?" or "What are you doing?"

Article IV. Disruptive Behaviors

There are a wide range of labels used to define children's disruptive behaviors. These are diagnostic labels imposed to provide mental health professionals, parents, and teachers with an "understanding" of why children behave as they do. These labels sometimes serve as an excuse for children's behaviors instead of focusing on change. For example, in response to a child's disruptive behavior, people often state, "Oh, he or she is attention deficit, bipolar, conduct disordered or hyperactive." This labeling process, when used to excuse behavior, identifies the child as "mentally ill" and therefore not as responsible for his or her actions. Glasser (2004), in his book, *Warning: Psychiatry Can Be Hazardous to Your Mental Health,* says that people are "mentally out of shape," not mentally ill," and that choice theory becomes the mental exercise needed to restore mental health. Dr. Glasser indicates that of the 465 mental illnesses identified by modern psychiatry there does not exist one medical test that can prove the existence of pathology. Diseases that do contribute to mental deterioration and have been medically proven as diseases of the brain include Parkinson's, Alzheimer's, and epilepsy. Dr. Fred A. Baughman, child neurologist and author of *The ADHD Fraud* (2006) supports this in a letter to Dr. William Glasser (personal communication):

The Psychiatric Times has given equal time to those who say psychiatric/mental *illnesses ARE real* diseases and those who say they ARE NOT. Whether disease is present or not is not a matter of vote or consensus, but whether or not, one patient at a time, a physical abnormality is demonstrable. Very simply, just as in medical school: abnormality = disease; no abnormality = normal = no disease. All physicians know this. We do not start insulin without proof of an elevated blood sugar. We do not surgically excise without proof of cancerous cells. We do not treat the thyroid without proof of subnormal thyroid hormone. What makes organized psychiatry's (American Psychiatric Association, American Academy of Child and Adolescent Psychiatry, National Alliance on Mental Illness, National Institute of Mental Health) claims of disease a total, 100%

fraud is that they never — I repeat — never, demonstrate, diagnose, prove, the presence of an objective abnormality within the brain or body of a single patient. They can't, they do no physical examinations or testing. Nonetheless, they call you and I, your relatives, neighbors, and friends, brain- "disordered"/"diseased"/"chemically imbalanced" and proceed to drug, shock, and perform psychosurgery upon us, often by court order, pronouncing that we are of diminished capacity, and a danger to ourselves and others. Believing them, failing to ask, for proof of an abnormality, the power we give them over us is totally arbitrary and inconsistent with the democratic ideals this country is based upon. Dr. James Scully, medical director of the APA, recently stated that emotional problems are in fact "brain diseases" and that this fact is as "incontrovertible as the Earth going round the sun." There being not a single mental/psychiatric "disorder"/"disease"/"chemical imbalance," verifiable in a single patient, I publicly charge that such claims are a total fraud against the American public. Further I charge that it is the responsibility of the PI (and all media) to demand of Dr. Scully and of all in organized psychiatry (APA, AACAP, NIMH, NAMI), the proof they must have to buttress their "disease" claims. Failing to do so, you become an accessory to this monstrous crime-in-progress (9 million U.S. schoolchildren are thus labeled and drugged today, increasingly by court-order, under threat of loss of custody).

Additional research in the area of ADHD also supports the lack of support for biological causes of this diagnosis as a brain illness. "Attempts to define a biological basis for ADHD have been consistently unsuccessful. The neuroanatomy of the brain, as demonstrated by neuroimaging studies, is normal" (Golden, 1991).

Children are often prescribed numerous medications to "alter the brain chemistry" and therefore change their behavior. This is especially true with the attention-deficit disorder (ADD)/hyperactivity label. Children are identified as ADD when they experience difficulties focusing on classroom tasks, cannot sustain attention to play activities, or when they do not seem to listen when spoken to directly. These identified behaviors are also characteristic of sexually abused children experiencing dissociative reactions to their abuse. These same children may experience high levels of anxiety and appear defiant in attempts to cope with their abuse and be labeled hyperactive, conduct disordered or oppositional-defiant. These children impulsively speak out and disrupt classroom learning and activities. They make frequent requests to leave the classroom to go to the bathroom, water fountain, or counselor's office. These actions by the child result when he is experiencing high anxiety, helplessness, and fear. In an attempt to reduce these emotional states, these children's motor activity increases and they attempt to distract themselves by acting out toward others, the teacher, or by self-injury. Some children may also try to escape environmental stimulation in large, noisy, or visually overstimulating classes through actions that remove them from the class or by asking to be excused. Some children will go so far as to behave in ways that they know will result in school suspensions to avoid feeling overstimulated in an environment that increases their feelings of low self-worth and destructive thinking processes. Intervention can be tricky because the goal is to reduce stimulation, which can be increased when too much emphasis is placed on talking and processing the situation. Discussions between the parent–teacher–therapist team can also evaluate whether optional learning environments that have smaller class sizes, less environmental stimulation, and an opportunity to learn and process information at an individualized pace would be more beneficial.

When children are diagnosed with a multitude of labels the next reaction by many psychiatrists and family physicians is to medicate with stimulants. It is commonly held that stimulants have a paradoxical effect on children compared to adults, but these drugs probably affect children and adults in the same way. At the doses usually prescribed by physicians, children and adults alike are "spaced out," rendered less in touch with their real feelings, and hence more willing to concentrate on boring, repetitive schoolroom tasks (Breggin & Breggin, 1995). Therefore these medications are considered desirable because they provide adults with more control over children. There are some questions that need to be pondered when presented with diagnostic labels.

1. What are the behaviors that resulted in this diagnosis?
2. What purpose do these behaviors serve the child (what basic need are they meeting)?
3. What factors may be contributing to these behaviors (abuse, neglect, parenting styles, etc.)?
4. What are some alternatives to helping children reduce their anxiety or increase attention span without drugs (responses to dissociation were discussed earlier in this chapter)?

Article V. Using Time-Out

In rare circumstances, time-outs may need to be employed to address disruptive behaviors. The purpose of this strategy is to teach children appropriate coping skills and encourage self-evaluation of disruptive behaviors. This may be used in any setting such as classrooms, groups, and at home.

Classroom time-outs can be within the class, which should be the first choice, or out-of-class in a supervised time-out room or counselors offices. Sometimes, allowing a child to excuse himself/herself to the restroom or water fountain can also obtain the same goal of calming him/her or reducing excess stimulation that they are responding to with high motor-activity or acting out. Time-out may be self-directed or at the teacher's suggestion. A minimum duration for the time-out may be established by the teacher or (ideally) determined by the students when they choose to return to the classroom tasks after their process of self-evaluation. Self-evaluation involves children calming themselves and formulating a plan that reduces their previously disruptive behavior. This plan may be shared with the teacher, therapist, or parent depending on the setting, or displayed through appropriate behavior.

Occasionally children may need to be directed to an out-of-class time-out when they do not choose to calm themselves or continue to be disruptive in the classroom. This should be considered a last option because it does not permit learning the current academic tasks that are being taught in the classroom. It also increases shame for many students that can actually increase the negative behaviors, especially when combined with the Seven Deadly Habits. Children during external classroom time-outs should be accompanied by an adult who helps children focus on their behavior, internally evaluate the behavior, and focus on new behaviors that do not produce negative consequences. This process can be achieved through the use of self-evaluation questions identified in chapter 1.

In his book, *Teach Them to Be Happy*, (1988), Sullo points out that time-out is typically utilized as a punishment strategy with young children in which the misbehaving child is cut off from activities and reinforcers. Once children have served the "sentence" they are allowed to rejoin the group (or family) no wiser, a bit more angry, and with self-esteem compromised. Utilizing time-out with choice theory encourages children to evaluate behavior, choose the time-out on their own, and how long they need to self-evaluate. In-class time-outs also do not disrupt children's ability to continue to learn because they are not removed from the learning environment. When time-out is used as a form of discipline in the home children are not restricted in their choices to play or have fun separately. For example, children who go to their room may read or play while calming themselves and before making a decision to return to the family activities. Younger children may require help in developing a plan; however, the time-out can still allow for a calming down period and self-reflection about why it may have been suggested.

Parent:	Thanks for taking the time in your room to calm down. Do you know what you did to need a time-out?
Child:	I threw my truck.
Parent:	That's right. You seemed to feel angry when I told you it was time to pick up your toys.
Child:	I didn't want to stop playing.
Parent:	I understand. I know you like to play. When it is time to pick up, though, do you think throwing your toys is the best way to express your anger?
Child:	No
Parent:	What might happen if you throw your things when you feel mad?
Child:	I don't know.
Parent:	Is it possible that you might break your toy or hurt someone if it hits them?
Child:	Yes
Parent:	Is this what you want to happen?
Child:	No
Parent:	Would you be willing to not throw your toys then when you are mad?
Child:	OK.

This dialogue suggests a way to discuss a possible disruptive behavior that often occurs with young children. It explores what happened, the consequence of possible outcomes, rearguing this type of behavior, and establishing a plan for future behavior.

Parents can also model self-directed time-out by indicating to the child that they are going to spend some time alone to deal with a frustrating situation and that they will talk with them when there has been enough time to think through the situation and make a plan of action. This encourages healthy coping behaviors.

Parent:	I need some time by myself to think about this situation. I need to calm down and organize my thoughts and how I want to respond.
Child:	I want an answer now.
Parent:	If I give you an answer without thinking it through I'm not sure I will make the best decision. I am going to the family room and I will be willing to talk about this in 30 minutes. Meet me back in the kitchen and I will talk more with you about what you want. Perhaps you will take this time to calm down too and then we can talk rationally about it.
Child:	Fine — 30 minutes.

When implementing strategies to deal with disruptive behaviors it is important to distinguish between punishment and discipline. Punishment usually involves coercion and frustrates all of the child's basic psychological needs of love and belonging, power, freedom and fun (Crawford, Bodine, & Hoglund, 2006). Punishment attempts to enforce rules for thinking and behavior through threats, manipulation, or force. Conversely, discipline encourages self-evaluation, self-control, and allows for natural and logical consequences. Thus, consequences are different from punishment in that they are known ahead of the behavior, imposed calmly, and are natural or related to the offense. Punishment is divulged after the behavior, imposed out of anger or frustration, and is often unrelated to the offense.

Therapists can help educate teachers, parents, and other caretakers on how to use discipline and avoid punishment. By avoiding punishment sexually abused children are less likely to suffer further damage to their self-worth (power within).

Article VI. Eating Difficulties

As was discussed in chapter 3, children sometimes choose to gain control over their emotional states and thinking processes through behaviors that cause self-harm and occasionally death. These attempts sometimes involve controlling food input and release from the body that has been labeled by the medical profession with terms such as *anorexia, bulimia,* and *compulsive overeating*. These actions are often accompanied by personal beliefs connected to a sexual abuse experience.

- Only I can control what someone can put in or take out of my body.
- I will no longer allow others to have power over my body.
- No one will ever make me do anything I don't want.

Among both adolescent girls and boys, a history of sexual abuse appears to increase the risk of disordered eating behaviors such as self-induced vomiting or use of laxatives to avoid gaining weight (Neumark-Sztainer et al., 2000). Other literature also suggests that sexually abused girls experience higher levels of emotional distress and have trouble coping. Food restriction and other disordered eating behaviors may reflect efforts to cope with such experiences (Wonderlich, et al., 1997). These types of self-harm behaviors reflect attempts to gain control over a physically and emotionally frightening experience. Some children attempt to make their bodies physically unattractive and avoid sexual attention in attempts to protect themselves from additional abuse. This may involve becoming excessively thin by undereating or becoming overweight through compulsive overeating. Sexual abuse victims also report that purging (bulimic activity) allows them to release pent-up emotions that result in them feeling calm and a sense of relief after the purge. This relief is only temporary, however, and therefore a cycle develops. In instances where bingeing occurs first, children may also attempt to regain their perception of control through purging. This behavior creates an illusion of power and control. These attempts to meet the need for power often bring attention to them by others who, because of concern, attempt to control the eating behaviors and perpetuate the problem. As children recognize that others are again attempting to take control over their bodies, they become more determined to continue the self-destructive patterns.

Counseling with choice theory helps children understand that they have developed creative and effective ways to meet the need for power. The focus is not on trying to make them eat, stop purging or overeating, but instead to develop their power within so that the current behaviors no longer are needed. It is important to dismiss that they are crazy or mentally ill but instead in need of help in developing healthy coping skills that do not conflict with the other psychological needs (survival, love and belonging, freedom, and fun). It also involves recognition that time will not be spent just focusing on what happened to them because choice theory emphasizes the here and now and only what the children do have control over, themselves. This is demonstrated through an initial session with Dee, age 13. Her parents brought her into counseling because they were concerned she was "anorexic." They reported she had been in counseling previously for three sessions (to focus on sexual abuse by a teen cousin); however the therapist terminated the case and informed them that Dee could not be helped unless she would discuss her sexual abuse. Dee told her parents that she would never see another counselor because she felt uncomfortable with having to talk when she did not want to. The family, prior to attending the first session was requested to have Dee seen for a medical checkup to determine whether her current eating patterns were resulting in medical problems. The family physician ruled out any physical difficulties that currently appeared connected to Dee's eating behaviors and agreed to collaborate as needed if Dee continued to lose weight. Dee's initial appointment included similar dialogue.

Therapist: Would you like to tell what brings you here today?
Dee: (angrily) I am not talking about Roger (the abusive cousin)! I am tired of everyone asking me about this!
Therapist: Wow, I can understand that. Actually I wanted to know what was going on "now" with you. I don't dig into people's pasts unless they think it is important.

Dee: (appears calmer and surprised). Really, then how are you going to help me? Everyone else seems to think I have problems because I was abused. My parents call me anorexic because I don't eat.

Therapist: Well Dee, you will figure out over time, that is, if you are willing to come back, that I think differently. My first thought is you don't eat because you have decided it helps you in some way.

Dee: So, you don't think I have problems because I was sexually abused?

Therapist: I believe that sexual abuse results in many emotions such as anger, fear, shame, and helplessness that people do their best to cope with. Sometimes the behaviors people use to deal with being upset over abuse are labeled problematic by others. What do you think about your eating?

Dee: I don't see it as a problem but my parents try to force and bribe me to eat — that makes me really upset!

Therapist: So, what do you do when your parents try these things?

Dee: Sometimes I eat to get them off my back or because I like what they are giving me, and other times I refuse. Now this really makes them mad and they ground me. But they can't make me do anything I don't want so sometimes I might eat a little, then I throw up — if they knew that I would really be in trouble. Are you going to tell them?

Therapist: No, I won't tell them because I don't think it would help, do you?

Dee: No, it would just make them madder and I wouldn't eat any more or less. So can you tell my parents to leave me alone about eating?

Therapist: I would be happy to talk to them if you would like. I would talk to them about not bugging you to eat because I don't think it helps either. Would that be ok?

Dee: Sure. So what is the catch?

Therapist: No catch. We will discuss making sure you have food available that you like to eat if you are hungry. How does that suit you?

Dee: Fine. I might even eat more if they would just leave it alone.

Therapist: Sounds like a plan. Would you be willing to come back again and talk to me about how this plan worked out? Also, maybe we can talk about how you deal with other stress in your life if you and your parents work this thing out and can argue less about food.

Dee: I'll come back as long as I don't have to talk about anything I don't want to.

Therapist: You don't have to talk about anything or do anything you don't
           want. I am not here to tell you what to do. My job is to help you
           with the things that are causing you to be unhappy and look at
           what you can do to feel better.
Dee: That sounds good.

The purpose of this session was to begin developing a relationship with
Dee where she understood she had choices and power within the counseling environment. Dee was the first to bring up the abuse or eating behaviors, not the therapist. The emphasis was on what she was doing now, not
the past, thereby building a foundation to discuss changes based on the
choice theory component of "acting" involved in total behavior. The parents were asked not to talk to Dee about food for the next week except to
ask what she wanted from the store. This reduced the power struggle. They
were agreeable to this. They were also asked to read the book *Unhappy
Teenagers* (Glasser, 2002). Additional appointments were set for Dee and
her parents separately in 1 week to discuss how the plan worked.

Article VII. Summary

Counseling sexually abused children will always involve addressing issues
of power. The emphasis is on increasing personal power, which has been
greatly affected by sexual abuse. Children need assistance in understanding that the abuse was not their fault and responsibility is placed on the
abuser. Reality therapy techniques, through the use of skillful questions
and strategies, can help focus on building strengths and increasing self-
evaluation to focus on changing their responses to sexual abuse. This is
a process that also involves increasing understanding and use of choice
theory concepts with those that support, care for, and provide learning to
the child. This type of environment provides the foundation for the child
to explore and take responsibility for her responses to sexual abuse while
building strengths and personal power. As positive approaches to dealing with negative beliefs and maladaptive behaviors are mastered, children
will begin to thrive and no longer view themselves as powerless. Power
is also achieved when children recognize that they have the freedom to
choose their responses to their abuse.

CHAPTER 6

Freedom of Choice

Freedom is an internal achievement, rather than an external adjustment.

Adam Clayton Powell

Freedom is that instant between when someone tells you to do something and when you decide how to respond.

Jeffrey Borenstein

The outward freedom that we shall attain will only be in exact proportion to the inward freedom to which we may have grown at a given moment.

And if this is the correct view of freedom, our chief energy must be concentrated upon achieving reform from within.

Gandhi

Freedom is a topic of interest worldwide. Most people refer to freedom in reference to "freedom to do." It is most evident when a person or group of people perceives that they are being denied the use of a set of behaviors they want to enact. Anyone who has ever parented a teen will most likely be accused of limiting freedom. People are even willing to die for the freedoms they want. Freedom, while highly valued, is often viewed in terms of external factors. External freedom refers to the material world of places, objects, and physical mobility. In contrast, internal freedom relates to an individual's world of thoughts, feelings, spirituality, and other intangibles.

Internal freedom, the ability to choose what to think and how to respond to the world, affects individuals' feelings and physiology and is essential for people to enjoy the external freedom they have. By the choices children make in response to their sexual abuse, they can significantly increase or decrease their external quality of life or freedom.

A sexual perpetrator violates the physical boundaries of children and may attempt to manipulate their emotional states to gain control. However, children can learn that they can choose their behaviors and thoughts related to their responses to sexual abuse. This is apparent based on the fact that children cope in many different ways. There are some external factors that may influence coping skills such as availability of support, resiliency factors (see chapter 2), or belief. However, children will ultimately determine what they do to deal with the aftermath of sexual abuse. In order for someone to change a coping skill they must take responsibility for making the choice and wanting to develop a new skill. This in no way takes any responsibility off the abuser for their behavior. Coping behaviors are not to be judged or externally evaluated by the therapist, only acknowledged as the best options that the person thought were available to him or her at the time.

Article I. Evaluating Choices

Counseling becomes a place where children can develop an understanding of the choices available to them and develop problem-solving skills to meet their basic needs more effectively.

Tamara, age 16, was referred for counseling by her mother. Tamara identified that her previous stepfather had sexually abused her for 2 years (ages 12–14). Tamara reported that they were currently waiting for a new trial date. Tamara stated the trial had been postponed and rescheduled three times over a 2-year period. The mother expressed concern that Tamara was "emotionally deteriorating" with every postponement. She stated that Tamara disclosed to Jenny, a teenaged friend, at age 14. Jenny's mother then contacted her (Tamara's mother) about the abuse. Tamara's mother said, "I did everything right." She believed her daughter, contacted the police, and divorced the offender. Initially, she stated that Tamara seemed to "continue on with her life" by going to school, and seemed to be happy and outgoing. The mother stated she began to observe changes in Tamara's behavior such as refusing to go to school and wanting to sleep more after the first trial postponement.

After the family had attended the initial session and had two additional postponements, Tamara quit school, began self-injury by cutting her arms, and was sleeping 12 to 16 hours a day. Tamara stated it was the court and the offender's fault that her life was so bad.

One aspect of working therapeutically with this family involved having Tamara examine the choices she was making in response to external factors such as court postponements, the offender, and school officials. The concept of "Freedom of Will" was addressed. Freedom of will means that we have the internal "freedom" to choose among various alternative actions available to us (Kawaljeet, 1999). Tamara was able to gradually identify that she had no control over other people or legal actions but could make choices that did not restrict her freedom. The "Helping or Hurting" table (see appendix for worksheet) demonstrates the internal evaluation by Tamara over several sessions.

This process involves Tamara identifying the choices she was making to cope and evaluating whether they were helping (increasing freedom and life choices) or hurting (restricting freedom and life choices). Tamara then identified new behaviors that she believed would help her feel more free, valuable, and in charge of her life. Tamara's most insightful moment came

Table 6.1 Helping or hurting?

Choice I am making now	Is this hurting or helping me?	Choices I would prefer to make	How will this help me?
1. Quitting school	Hurting	Graduate from high school	More job opportunities. Feel proud of myself
2. Sleeping too much	Hurting	Spend time doing things I enjoy such as planting flowers, seeing friends, getting a job	I'll feel less depressed and live my life instead of sleeping it away
3. Cutting on arms	Hurting	Find new ways to reduce stress	Mom will quit worrying so much, which makes me feel better
4. Avoiding friends	Hurting	Calling my friends to hang out	I will have more fun and think less about the trial
5 Fighting with Mom	Hurting	Be able to talk about my anger instead of taking it out on Mom	I will feel closer to mom again. We will both be happier and less stressed

toward the end of treatment when she stated, "I put myself in a prison waiting for him (the offender) to go to jail. I don't want to suffer for what he did to me, I want him to suffer." The revelation by Tamara demonstrates how sexual abuse victims can restructure their thought processes and become aware that they have the freedom to choose their response to sexual abuse.

Traditional problem solving involves, (1) identifying a problem; (2) brainstorming solutions; then (3) putting into action the best possible choice. Steps one and two remain the same when using a reality therapy approach. The process varies slightly in reality therapy because clients are asked to evaluate the effectiveness of their choice of behaviors or thought processes. Once effective behaviors are identified, they are put into action. This is done to help children so that they can thrive when they have numerous choices to meet each of their psychological needs.

Article II. Creating New Options

It is important to create as many options as possible to meet the basic needs. This helps create new pictures or to refocus existing pictures within the child's quality world. It allows for flexibility in the event one path or option becomes blocked by external or internal factors. For example, children who have only one friend may suffer more loss of love and belonging if that person moves away or chooses not to be their friend than children who may have several friends in their quality world. Likewise, the child whose self-worth is primarily determined by gymnastics may find difficulty coping if there are no other sources to meet the need for power should an injury occur. This philosophy is exemplified in the statement, "Don't put all your eggs in one basket." One way to examine where options need to be created is through a writing exercise that identifies what the basic needs are and how they could be met. The exercise below "Meeting My Needs" (see appendix for worksheet) is for children to identify a minimum of three ways to meet each basic need. The following was completed during a session with Tamara.

Some children may be unrealistic about what they want to do. They are asked to evaluate whether the resources and skills are available to obtain what they want. For example, a child who at age 12 wants to race cars would be limited by the inability to obtain a driver's license. All options, however, should be acknowledged for the need they would meet. It is up to children and caregivers to evaluate whether the resources (talent, grades, financial) are easily available. Options may also be examined for conflict behavior and the needs re-evaluated in some circumstances. For example, gangs can meet the need for love and belonging but conflict with the need for freedom when children are placed in detention centers for illegal gang

Table 6.2 Meeting my needs

Survival	Love & belonging	Power	Freedom	Fun
Lock the doors in my house	Spend more time with mom shopping or helping around the house	Get my GED	Stop letting postponements control my life	Joke around more with mom again and fight less with her
Don't hurt my body with drugs or cutting	Call my friends to hang out	Work on my flower beds, which everyone always compliments me on	Ask for what I want — a work shift transfer	Go skating with my friends
Tell my mom if I see my stepdad (offender) in our neighborhood	Go back to work	Realize I am going to be OK and tell myself this every time I "get down" about court postponements	Get out of bed and enjoy life instead of hiding in bed	Walk my dog in the park

behavior. By helping develop many alternatives to meet their needs, children increase their freedom through choices. The use of self-evaluating questions and humor can be useful in examining possibilities. These techniques can help reduce children's perceptions that their ideas are being criticized or their brainstorming not respected.

Nate, age 6, was referred to anger management counseling following a disclosure of sexual abuse by his 14-year-old half-brother. The biological father, Sam, had emergency custody because the biological mother refused to have the 14-year-old half-sibling placed with another relative. A juvenile hearing was scheduled to determine if the teen offender would be placed in boys school. Nate stated at the intake that he was sad and angry that Andrea (he referred to his biological mother by her given name) did not believe the "yucky things" his brother did to him. Nate disclosed how he was getting into trouble for hitting people at school and home. He had a 4-year-old full sibling and a 10-year-old stepbrother in his father's home. He reported wanting to make people "pay" when they made him mad. He stated he didn't like getting into trouble though because he would have to miss recess at school and Dad would take his PlayStation away at home.

As a result of Nate's decision to express his feeling of anger by hurting others, he was losing external freedom. Some of his behaviors were also moving toward bullying (see section on "Bullying and Aggression" later in this chapter), and he needed to learn new behaviors and thought processes to respond to his internalized anger. This was addressed by discussions that anger was an appropriate feeling for what he was dealing with, including the abuse, disbelief by the mother, and actions by others at school and at home; however, he did not have to harm others to release this anger. Nate was initially emotionally guarded, possibly as a result of fears regarding disbelief, identified embarrassment about the abuse, and a new relationship with this therapist. Therefore, humor was used regularly with Nate during discussions about alternative behaviors to meet his need for power. Nate would frequently brainstorm behaviors to cope with his anger that he appeared to recognize as having negative consequences (freedom reducing). This may have been because he was unable to generate positive ideas or his way of using humor with the therapist to limit-test. Regardless, it was important to maintain a nonjudgmental response, and humor was productive in encouraging Nate to generate more freedom-producing behaviors.

Therapist: Referencing two pictures from a drawing exercise (see Appendix for worksheets) "Something That I Get Angry About" and "What I Do When Angry." Nate, can you tell me what's going on in these pictures?

Nate: (pointing) Can't you tell by looking?

Therapist: Well, Nate, I'm getting a little old and I don't see as well as I did at one time. It would really help me if you could tell me about your drawings.

Nate: (laughing) OK, this one is my brother not letting me play with the PlayStation. And this one is me kicking him in the head.

Therapist: Wow, can you kick that high?

Nate: (laughing) Yes.

Therapist: What would happen if you kicked him in the head? Would you get what you want?

Nate: No, and Dad would probably not let me play for a long time. That's what happened when I hit Gary. Dad hid it but I found it and he got even madder.

Therapist: (looking thoughtful) Nate, I was wondering, is there something else you might be able to do if you want to also play with the PlayStation that wouldn't make your Dad decide to play hide and seek with it?

Nate: (laughing again) I could tell Dad I want to play with it.

Therapist: (applauding) Yea Nate!

Nate: (smiling)

Therapist: (serious mood) Hold on. Now would asking Dad cause him to punish you and hide the PlayStation?

Nate: (rolling his eyes) No!

Therapist: Nate, I'd like to ask your permission to discuss a PlayStation sharing schedule with your dad. Do you think this would help?

Nate: (looking pleased) That would be good.

Therapist: I'd like to tell you how proud I am that you were able to come up with a new way to get what you want when you feel angry that doesn't cause problems for you. Do you think we could talk about more ideas like this another time?

Nate: Sure.

This dialogue demonstrates how humor can appropriately be utilized when brainstorming new behaviors that can bypass client limit-testing without judgmental responses by the therapist.

Article III. "Freedom To" and "Freedom From"

There are two types of freedom everyone has. "Freedom to" refers to the need to make independent choices regarding acting and thinking. "Freedom from" refers to the avoidance of physical and emotional pain and avoidance of boredom. Therapy can increase "freedom to" by identifying choices. In the counseling sessions, the child may choose where to sit, be able to choose between a variety of therapeutic games, and choose what to or what not to talk about.

In the group counseling modality, children can have "freedom to" help establish group expectations, pick partners for activities, pick between activities, utilize the time-out area, and help plan a final party celebration.

"Freedom from" needs to exist in any counseling modality, which includes freedom from criticism, punishment, violence, fear, and boredom. A counselor who practices the seven caring habits and promotes fun (see chapter 6) will ensure a healthy environment that provides freedom.

People are free when they can make choices that do not hurt others or themselves. Empowerment and a sense of freedom also occur as knowledge about how to identify and avoid potentially abusive situations. Children can become fearful of adults, peers, being alone, darkness, going to sleep, or any other situation that triggers concerns about revictimization. Helping children increase awareness of their personal safety enables them to gain confidence through knowing they have choices about how to deal with these fears.

Fear of adults, peers, or situations where they perceive they have little freedom of choice, is common in sexually abused children. Some specific concepts that can be taught in counseling are good versus bad secrets, bribes, tattling versus telling, and personal rights.

Article IV. Good Secrets vs. Bad Secrets

When children are sexually abused, the offender often engages the child in sharing the situation as a secret. This is especially common when the child has a close relationship with the abuser. Children are often confused about whether it is OK to tell a secret because they have been taught that secrets are special situations that people entrust them with. There are two useful ways to help children with sorting out whether it is OK to tell a secret or not. The process begins with discussing that people sometimes attempt to trick children by asking them to keep a secret. It is important to reinforce that even if the child kept the secret for a period of time that the abuse was not their fault. Help them understand that the other person is at fault for tricking them. Explain that you will help them begin to try to figure out how to deal with the situations that involve secrets.

Section 4.01 Technique 1

Let the child know you are going to identify a situation and you would like for them to identify whether they consider it a good secret or a bad secret. Take the time to discuss each one after they have answered. Some examples include:

1. What you are giving your Mom for her birthday.
2. A surprise party for your brother or sister.
3. Someone wants to touch your private parts.
4. Someone put a fake spider in the teacher's desk.
5. Someone shows you a picture of someone who is naked.
6. Someone wants you to take off your clothes so they can take pictures of you.
7. Dad is going to take Mom to a special dinner.

Section 4.02 Technique 2

This involves discussing a scenario that involves elements of coercion or manipulation. For example: "A little boy/girl is staying all night at a friend's house. The friend's daddy has always been very nice and knows the child's parents very well. The daddy, after the friend goes to sleep, offers to show the child a movie where people take off their clothes and touch each other. The daddy also wants to do what the people in the movie are doing with the child. The daddy tells the child that if they do these things, then he will take them to the toy store the next day and he does. The child agrees to the behaviors. The daddy says, "Let's keep this our secret and you can keep the toy." The child says he or she will keep the secret. Is this a good secret or a bad secret?

These types of techniques may also be useful in situations where another child committed the abusive act. Parents, teachers, and other adults often discourage tattling, which frequently is a problematic behavior between children. Children need information that helps them distinguish tattling from telling. This discussion is useful in conjunction with a "good secrets vs. bad secrets" discussion. The biggest difference between tattling and telling is that telling involves wanting to stop a behavior that infringes on another person's rights to safety, personal space, or boundaries. Tattling exists only to obtain punishment for another person. Again, a list may be provided and discussed with the child in identifying different behaviors as tattling or telling:

- Someone touches your private parts.
- Dad ate the last cookie.
- A sibling makes funny faces or sticks out his or her tongue.
- Being asked to take off your clothes by the babysitter
- A teacher asks to take pictures of you and not tell.

Regardless of any given situation, children who feel confident about decision making will feel empowered and a sense of personal freedom when they can identify choices and make good decisions for their personal safety.

Fears can emotionally and physically immobilize a child. Sexual abuse often results in fears of the dark, revictimization, and retaliation because of disclosure. In order to control a child, an offender may threaten his or her personal safety or the safety of those close to the child. Children may be told they will be hurt, punished, not loved, disbelieved, and even killed if they disclose the abuse. In other situations, children may develop fears without overt threats. This often occurs when children are aware of additional abusive behaviors such as domestic violence toward self or others. There is a logical connection drawn between what the abuser has done to harm others nonsexually and what he or she is capable of doing to the child. Prior to and following a disclosure, children may exhibit fears of the dark or sleeping alone because these are vulnerable situations in which the child perceives he or she is powerless and has limited choices for protection.

Natasha, age 8, was sexually abused by her stepfather for 3 years, and she was brought to counseling because of her fears of sleeping alone, darkness, and retaliation by her stepfather. Her mother described a ritual that Natasha went through every night before bed. It involved checking that all doors and windows in the home were locked and checking under her bed and in the closet in her room to be sure that no one was hiding. Natasha also reported she wanted to sleep with a light on and sometimes wanted to sleep with her mother. The mother reported that since they had moved she only had a twin bed for herself and that her daughter sleeping with her in the bed was not conducive to a good night's sleep. Natasha's stepfather, who currently was not incarcerated while awaiting trial, had been physically abusive to the mother and had made threats that he or his friends would get even for the sexual abuse charges. Counseling helped both Natasha and her mother to recognize that Natasha's behavior was not unrealistic and that it provided the child with the opportunity to try and ensure her own safety. The mother was encouraged to allow the safety check behaviors, thereby not removing Natasha's efforts to self-protect and make choices that reduced anxiety. Sleeping arrangements were negotiated between Natasha and her mother that included a night light, and that Natasha, if fearful or anxious upon waking in the middle of the night, could quietly go to the mother's room and sleep in a sleeping bag next to her mother's bed.

Some children make choices in dealing with their fears that harm others. Boys who have been taught to be "tough" or not to appear powerless sometimes determine the best way to feel less victimized is to become the victimizer. These behaviors don't exclude girls but are more prevalent among males. They include bullying behaviors, sexual activity, acting out, and frequent fighting. These types of behaviors all temporarily reduce negative beliefs developed as a result of sexual abuse (see chapter 5). Children can learn that they are free to make and learn new behaviors and thinking patterns that also result in feeling empowered, but that don't result in harm to others. This process involves learning positive problem solving and choosing to take charge of their lives. A part of examining thinking patterns that decrease and increase freedom is to examine the words clients use when speaking. For example:

Section 4.03 Decrease Freedom

should	uncontrollable	must
have to	inevitable	can't
destined	unavoidable	won't

Section 4.04 Increase Freedom

choose	could/can	try
attempt	possible	workable

When someone uses words that increase freedom, they are able to see more possibilities and generate new alternatives for coping. In the children's movie, *Alice in Wonderland,* Alice is speaking to the rabbit about how she will possibly fit into a small passageway. The rabbit indicates it is "impassible" and Alice comments, "impossible." The rabbit replies by telling her, "Nothing is impossible." This change in thinking results in Alice considering possible options (drinking a potion that shrinks her) to obtain her goal. If Alice had only looked at the situation as impossible she would not have had the idea to try something new. Counseling can help children to confront what seems to be an impossible situation by teaching them to identify new coping strategies that allow them to deal with both self-imposed and imposed obstacles.

Article V. Bullying and Aggression

Bullies are often children experiencing life situations, such as sexual abuse, that resulted in their feeling helpless and out of control. In their attempts to cope with stress and feeling of powerlessness, they impose obstacles that limit their "freedom to" and "freedom from." They typically have poor social skills and view themselves as unable to live up to other people's expectations. Therefore, bullies seek to regain their feelings of power, competence, and control over their own lives by harming or intimidating other children. Bullies tend to think in terms of words that decrease freedom, which further frustrates them and fuels the bullying behaviors. Physical behaviors often include hitting, kicking, shoving, taking money or other forms of extortion, and tripping. Boys usually engage in physical bullying; however, girls are not excluded from acts of physical bullying. Bullying by girls can take alternate psychological forms such as spreading rumors, social exclusions, and ridicule about physical appearance. These emotional strategies serve the same purpose as physical bullying, which is to hurt, damage self-esteem, control and manipulate other children. Bullying is a repetitive activity. These behaviors only empower bullies for a short period of time and must be ongoing for them to overcome their own thoughts and feeling of powerlessness.

In addition to sexual abuse as a factor, which bullies may have in their history, these children may also be experiencing additional environmental factors that encourage violence.

- Domestic violence
- Physical and emotional abuse
- Being bullied
- Violent television viewing
- Violent Internet or video games

Bullying has begun to receive more attention through media coverage of school shootings and children carrying weapons to school both for the purpose of intimidation and self-protection. This increase in awareness has resulted in more research into bullies and not just their victims. Bullies are generally older, have positive attitudes toward violence, experience low anxiety, feel secure, and have average self-esteem. They display little empathy for victims, have been exposed to aggressive models and misperceive intents of others as hostile (Batsche & Knoff, 1994). They are quick to anger, impulsive, and disorganized. They provoke or irritate peers, fight back when attacked, and offer exaggerated anger responses (Schwartz, Proctor, & Chien, 2001). It is important to begin understanding how to treat the bullies because childhood bullying can lead to involvement in gang activities and a criminal record (Borg, 1999).

A successful approach in therapy with bullies involves many dimensions, which involves the child with the bullying behaviors, the therapist, and the family of the child and his teachers. The James H. Bean School in Sidney, Maine, which is K-5, has received national recognition for its bullying prevention program. This program is based on the research of Norway's Dr. Daniel Olweus. The Bean School began its bullying prevention program coordinated by school counselor Stan Davis in 1998, and has built a discipline system that focuses on problem solving and applying consequences that are nonhostile, predictable, fair, and immediate. Stan Davis has incorporated the ideas that he implemented at the James H. Bean Elementary School in his book, *Schools Where Everyone Belongs* (2005). Instead of critical responses, bullies are asked to complete a "Think about It" form following aggressive behaviors. (A detailed "Think about It" form is included in the appendix). This self-evaluation includes a series of questions that help children acknowledge their actions, discover and feel the effect of those actions on others, and find new ways to reach the goals they were working toward through the aggressive actions. These questions include:

1. What did you do?
2. Why was that the wrong thing to do?
3. What problem(s) were you trying to solve?
4. Next time you have this problem, how will you solve it without hurting anyone?

Therapy involves having children who bully examine their behavior. As therapists, the role is to show that someone cares enough to make the bully face a truth that he has spent his life trying to avoid, and emphasizes that he is responsible for his behaviors (Glasser, 1989). It is important to establish an environment where the bully is held accountable but without fear of criticism of other self-esteem-reducing techniques. The emphasis in office-based counseling will involve social skills and empathy development (see chapter 4), problem solving with nonaggressive actions, reduction of environmental aggression, stress reduction techniques (see chapter 3), and caretaker involvement. Collaborations with school teachers and administrators are critical in reduction of school-based bullying. A comprehensive website for school personnel about bullying can be found at http://www.stopbullyingnow.com.

It is essential to involve caretakers in the treatment of sexually abused children. This involvement serves many purposes. First, it allows therapists to educate caretakers in the use of strategies and behaviors that are nonpunitive and consistent and which address aggressive and bullying behaviors. Second, because many children who bully come from home situations where there is little warmth, minimal positive adult attention, and in which discipline is inconsistent and periodically emotionally and physically aggressive, these caretakers also need to learn new behaviors (Olweus, 1993). Caretaker involvement is also necessary in order to reduce an important third possible contributor to bullying. This possible contributor is aggressive television and video games. A review of literature (Anderson & Bushman, 2002), indicates a positive correlation between violent video game playing and aggressive behaviors. Therefore, requesting that the caretakers temporarily stop children from watching aggressive television programs and using violent video/Internet games can be helpful during treatment to reduce aggressive behaviors. As children mature emotionally, reduce aggressive behaviors, and begin to understand the difference between simulated and real aggression, then parents can gradually reintroduce programming or gaming they consider appropriate. Requesting that caretakers remove items such as televisions, computers, and even violent music from their children's rooms will also allow the adults to be more aware of their children's activities. Johnson and Gil (1992) suggest in their book *Sexualized Children: Assessment and Treatment of Sexualized Children and Children Who Molest* that sexually abused children can be stimulated to sexually act out by viewing television and movies that contain scenes of violence. Therefore, these types of restrictions serve multiple purposes in treatment.

When caretakers reduce environmental stimulants for aggression, children can focus on new options, therefore being able to both increase "freedom to" and "freedom from." "Freedom to" will include their opportunities to develop new and healthy relationships, and awareness of more behavioral possibilities to cope with stress, anger, powerlessness. Their "freedom from" punishment, fear, negative self-beliefs, and criticism will also increase their quality of life.

Article VI. Focusing on Controllable Situations

When referred to counseling for anger management or other acting out behaviors toward others, children need to learn that they are capable of choosing other options to deal with their emotions. In addition to examining how all the basic needs are being met, the process of making decisions to change harmful behaviors can be achieved through decision making. Begin by identifying, with the child's input, circumstances within or out of a person's control. Typically, they will be able to be summed up into a few categories.

Section 6.01 Conditions That Can Be Controlled

- Our behavior
- Our thinking processes
- How we choose to feel
- Physiological responses

Section 6.02 Conditions That Can't Be Controlled

- Anything another person does, thinks, feels, or physiologically responds to
- Genetic abnormalities
- Terminal illnesses

With these parameters established, the child can begin to focus on making changes in them. Begin by discussing choices made on a regular basis. This begins by developing awareness that all behaviors are chosen. A worksheet exercise that can be used individually or in a group setting is "Choices I Made Today" (see appendix for worksheet). Even the simplest behaviors are reviewed (brushing teeth, getting up when the alarm rings, or when Mom told me to, eating breakfast, etc.) Identifying the choices made on a regular or daily basis is a part of learning and understanding problem solving. The next stage involves examining needs and wants and self-evaluating (see "Meeting My Needs" worksheet in the appendix). Asking questions or providing questions encourages self-evaluation and elicits possible solutions that may already exist in the child's repertoire. Review the following exchange.

Dan: I am always getting kicked out of school for fighting.

Therapist: Is that what you want to happen?

Dan: No, it makes things even worse.

Therapist: What have you been doing to make this situation better?

Dan: I try not to get mad but people can really get on my nerves and then I have to hit them.

Therapist: So, your only option is to hit someone when they get on your nerves?

Dan: I've walked away a few times. It just wasn't worth getting suspended.

Therapist: So, what you are telling me is that you do have control whether you hit someone. It's just sometimes worth it and other times it isn't?

Dan: Yeah, I just need to not get so angry.

Therapist: What would you think if I told you that you could still feel just as angry but choose to do something different?

Dan: I might agree, but I'm not sure I can always do it.

Therapist: Are you willing to try?

Dan: If it will keep me from getting suspended.

Therapist: We can talk about ways to reduce how you are feeling and change how you act when you are angry, if you want. Are you willing to continue looking at things you can do differently?

Dan: I'll try.

Therapist: That's all I am asking.

This initial dialogue demonstrates several components necessary to discuss problem solving. First, it avoids "Why" questions, which are judgmental and deter good problem solving. Second, the therapist asked, "What have you been doing to make the situation better?" This implies that the child has the ability to form decisions and that possible solutions exist. Third, it incorporates choice theory education that encourages the child to understand that behaviors are a matter of choice. Finally, it begins to examine that new possibilities exist for a plan and a request for commitment to examine change is obtained. Following this, counseling will involve identifying available resources and alternatives to coping with anger.

Article VII. Summary

An important aspect of counseling using choice theory involves teaching children that they have the "freedom to" make new choices, learn new skills, and how to increase their "freedom from" future abuse. Therapists, by focusing on internal freedom, help children gain empowerment and enjoy more external freedoms such as play and social interactions.

CHAPTER 7

Fun, Curiosity, and Sexual Development

"Play is the highest expression of human development in childhood, for it alone is the free expression of what is in a child's soul. "

Friedrich Froebel, "Father" of the modern kindergarten

Fun is not an optional part of the healing process, it is one of its chief rewards (Bass & Davis, 1988). As children become able to identify the effects of sexual abuse and develop efficient skills to meet all their needs, they will experience more joy and fun in their lives. Counseling expands awareness of new resources and provides information to cope effectively with sexual abuse. Children learn valuable skills through their experiences with fun during social interactions. Playing with others is need fulfilling. Play provides love and belonging because it involves others who typically share common interests, power through learning activities, and opportunities to demonstrate skills and freedom to make decisions about whether or how to be involved in the interactions of playing. Fun, however, is often neglected or denied in the sexually abused child's world. Children may be overwhelmed by emotions such as fear, confusion, shame, and trying to figure out how to cope when sexual abuse takes place. They may withdraw from previously enjoyable activities such as playing with others, hobbies, and schoolwork. Their negative beliefs (see chapter 5) about themselves can result in depressing thoughts and behaviors that also result in other children withdrawing from them. Under these circumstances, a child may even switch peer groups in order to identify with other children who do not think positively about themselves. These peer groups can include gangs where the need for fun is met through self-destruction and conflicts with other people's needs. Children who at one time met their need for fun by playing or engaging in cooperative play, activities that are socially acceptable, and achieved in school, may decide that disruptive classroom behaviors (chapter 5), bullying (chapter 6), and vandalism are more fun.

It is unusual for a child to be referred to counseling due to parental or educational providers' concerns about whether a child is experiencing fun. When a reason for a referral is carefully examined, it will be apparent in some situations that the child is experiencing difficulties with meeting their need for fun. For example:

"My child is crying all the time."
"My child refuses to go to school."
"My child is running with a gang."
"My child has quit all her previous hobbies."
"My child is withdrawn/isolated from everyone."

In the above examples, the reasons for referral are directly related to whether or how a child is meeting his or her need for fun. As a child learns how to meet all the basic needs effectively through counseling, he or she will begin to experience fun, efficient behaviors.

Counseling should attempt to provide a need-fulfilling environment in which a child and caretakers can experience fun while healing from sexual abuse. Some possible ways to achieve this in counseling are humor, games and activities, and opportunities to fulfill all the basic needs through efficient behaviors.

Article I. Therapeutic Humor

Fun and enjoyment may be the most neglected need for children and their caretakers when coping with sexual abuse. Sexual abuse is a very serious situation that should never be minimized or not taken seriously. However, when children and caretakers learn that all of their basic needs must be fulfilled additional frustrations can occur. With this information they may be willing to accept that they can deal with the sexual abuse and still allow for times to experience fun through appropriate humor and fun activities. Parents or caretakers will most likely agree that they are better at their caretaking responsibilities when they have moments of fun. It is important to give the family permission to experience fun and humor in the middle of a nonjoyous crisis. Sultanoff (1992) outlines several criteria for using humor effectively within the counseling setting. It requires that the counselor:

1. Have planned humor in his or her repertoire.
2. Be willing to risk using the humor.
3. Have assessed the client's level of humor and his or her ability to accept humorous interventions.
4. Be prepared to respond to the client's reaction to the humor.
5. Be capable of taking him- or herself lightly and his or her work seriously.
6. Use humor that is genuine and congruent with whom the counselor is as a person.

Research into the use of humor with participants indicates that the experience of humor can positively influence a person's state of hopelessness. Humor may competitively inhibit negative thoughts by substituting positive ones, and thereby foster hope in individuals (Vilaythong, Arnau, Rosen, & Mascaro, 2003). Positive emotions can stimulate thought and prompt people to discard inefficient behavioral responses and pursue more creative paths of thought and action. Laughter is a total behavior process that has also been found to lower blood pressure, reduce stress hormones, and boost immune functions by raising levels of infection-fighting T-cells. Laughter also triggers the release of endorphins, the body's natural pain-killers, and produces a general sense of well-being. Life events such as sexual abuse have an effect on emotions and moods that can directly impact our immune systems. A sense of humor results in positive emotions, which create neurochemical changes that can counteract the stress, placed on the body by the emotional aspect of coping with sexual abuse.

When used appropriately, counselors can utilize humor to provide some relief from life situations that may otherwise seem unbearable. Increased bonding between therapists and clients helps to reinterpret distressing events that can aid in distancing children and caretakers from the abuse, thus providing a different perspective. Use of humor by the child or caretakers within the counseling situation may also indicate an increasing sign of mental health, strength and connectedness with the counselor. As with all therapeutic interventions the counselor must ask him- or herself, "How will this humor help my client?" The counselor must avoid gratifying his or her own need to be humorous and focus on how humor will be helpful to the client (Sultanoff, 1992). Other cautions about using humor are suggested by Dunkelblau (1999).

1. Beware of sarcasm and abrasive humor.
2. Be aware of your own emotions. Sometimes humor is a left-handed way of expressing your own anger and aggression.
3. Be cautious about clients feeling they are not being taken seriously.
4. Humor must always be used to facilitate, not interrupt the healing process.

Group counseling offers many opportunities to create fun in the counseling environment. Regardless of age, playing can be incorporated into group sessions. The emphasis will be on cooperative games that emphasize participation, fun, and interactions. Games can be used to problem solve, encourage group connectedness, and empower the participants. In groups such as child/teen sexual abuse or caretakers of sexually abused children, games may be used to break down inhibitions that result from anxiety about interacting with people they do not know or because of fear of shame resulting from sexual abuse. Group activities also involve sharing ideas and personal information that can set the tone for relationship building, which increases the commitment level and can help bring about a successful outcome of group effectiveness.

Article II. Icebreaker Activities in Groups

These group exercises reduce stress, promote social skills, and increase group connectedness. It is fun to begin or end a group session with one of these activities.

Section 2.01 Interview

Members are divided into pairs. The therapist can participate if an odd number of group members exist. Each person asks (interviews) the other a set of predetermined questions about interests, hobbies, etc. Then they switch roles. After each group member completes a turn as interviewer, everyone returns to the group, introduces their partner and shares the partner's responses to the questions with the rest of the group.

Section 2.02 Bingo

Each group member is provided with a Bingo card and asked to find a group member who matches the description in one of the boxes. The first person to obtain five (5) names in a row (horizontally, vertically, or diagonally) obtains Bingo.

Section 2.03 Toilet Paper Game

This can be utilized in individual, group, or family therapy and in parent/child education groups. A roll of toilet paper is passed to each person who is participating. Each child or adult is asked to pull off as much toilet paper as they want. Next, each person will separate the toilet paper into individual sections. Then each person is asked to write one nice thing about him- or herself on each section of toilet paper. Then, going around in a circle, the compliments or strengths that each person has listed are read out loud. Another variation when working with families is to ask each person to write positive statements about the other family members.

Section 2.04 Gossip

This may be done in one small group or, when working with larger groups of people, broken down into more than one group. The game begins when the first person in a group chooses a prewritten statement from a bowl. Some ideas are: "I heard that she was going to break up her friends' relationship," or "The boys plan to sneak out and go toilet paper the nice principal's house." The first person then whispers the statement to the person next to them. That person will whisper the statement to the next person and so on. Each person is allowed to say the statement only one time. The last person to hear the statement then writes it on a board or is asked to repeat the gossip aloud. It is always interesting to discuss how perceptions can alter the final statement from the original one.

Section 2.05 Web String Toss

Have everyone sit in a circle. One person begins by locating the end of the yarn ball and tossing it to another group member. The person who catches it may be asked a question by the tosser about interests, favorite things such as color, food, vacations, or any other nonthreatening questions. This person then holds on to a portion of the yarn and tosses it to another person thus continuing the cycle. This is continued until everyone has had an opportunity to ask and be asked at least one question. A parallel can be made between the pieces of yarn that cross and connect and the common interests that the group has, as well as the new connections being made.

Section 2.06 Have You Ever?

The group is asked to form a circle with their chairs with only enough chairs for each person minus one. The facilitator may choose to start without a seat and stand in the middle of the circle. This game then begins by the person in the middle asking, "Have you ever _____?" Everyone who has ever _____ then gets up and moves to another chair, including the person in the middle. This will leave one person without a chair who begins the next round of "Have you ever _____?" This is a great high energy and fun activity to get a group started or to give a boost to a group halfway through a session.

Playing games can help to reduce inhibitions of group members and prepare participants to engage in the process of change and willingness to share self-evaluations with others. Games can also accentuate the group theme for a session by structuring activities such as web string toss (love and belonging) or toilet paper game (power play), which involve natural curiosity and includes sexual exploration by children. Like many other areas of children's lives, sexual development is impacted by the sexual abuse experience.

Article III. Normal Sexual Development

On their own, children will normally engage in playful and explorative activities. Sometimes these activities will involve normal curiosity and include sexual exploration. Sexual abuse disrupts normal sexual development and may lead to a variety of early sexual behaviors.

Beginning shortly after birth, children will begin to exhibit natural curiosity about their bodies. By the age of 5 months, children may begin to touch their private parts because it feels pleasurable or provides a relaxing response. Male children will exhibit penile erections and females will produce vaginal lubrication in response to touch. Between 12 and 18 months children will continue masturbation activities and begin to give and want to receive mutual affection. Gender identity also begins to develop and they may begin to show some early interest in the genders of other children or adults as they grasp the physical differences between males and females. Gender role identity is a combination of biological and societal influences. Roles are strongly influenced by expectations of the culture and familial beliefs the child lives within. Everything from clothing, toys chosen to play with, early career ideas, or extracurricular activities is influenced by gender role socialization.

During the years between ages 2 and 5, children's interest in the genitals of playmates increases and interest in playing "doctor" or "mommy and daddy" may develop. Children within this age group usually exhibit minimal modesty and enjoy being naked, "streaking," or exposing their body parts. This age span is an opportune time to begin discussions of what "private" means, as well as the correct names for the anatomical parts of the genitals or breasts. Privacy issues can be discussed in regard to masturbating activities, boundaries with children's bodies and other people's, and good/bad touch or good/yucky secrets. Children need to know appropriate vocabulary, such as penis, vagina, rectum, breasts, urination, or bowel movement in order to correctly communicate with parents, caregivers, teachers, or physicians when discussing their physical problems or even sexual abuse.

Between the ages of 6 and 11 (the elementary school years) children become exposed to a wider range of influences as a result of contact with peers who have a different knowledge base and environmental factors that affect sexual socialization. During this age range, children are also exposed to a wider range of influences such as television, videos, and media, books, and magazines that introduce new information that affects emerging attitudes and behaviors about sexuality.

Parental behaviors, such as type of sexual behavior exhibited in the home, clothing choices, language about sexuality and people's behaviors and attitudes they allow around their children, all influence sexual socialization in children. Parents should always be aware that their behaviors speak louder than their words. An exception to this may be when sexual expressions are used in anger.

Boys and girls begin to notice each other's physical differences even more during the elementary school years. Some children will begin to have physical indicators or experience early signs of puberty such as body hair, pimples, and body odor. A small percentage of females will begin to menstruate by the end of this age span. Children usually continue to explore their own bodies through self-stimulation or mutual masturbation. These activities may appear to diminish based on parental reporting because of increased modesty, fear of ridicule, or punishment. An increase in covert sexual expressions through jokes, dirty language, or play (such as young boys who grab each others' private areas in playful behaviors), and exploration of creative ways to masturbate (rubbing on stuffed animals or objects, running water on genitals) also is considered natural and healthy.

As children enter middle school at about age 11 or 12, proceed through high school, and enter into adulthood, sexual development is very active. Children become more conscious of societally imposed gender roles and often are teased or punished by peers or family for violations from the norm. As a result of hormonal changes, children become more focused on their own bodies and those of others. Sexual experimentation such as hugging, kissing, fondling, and in some cases, intercourse will begin to occur in early puberty. Children may also experiment with same gender sexual play. This early experimentation does not mean that the child is homosexual. It usually results because of opportunity and within peer groups. Because of the numerous influences of sexuality on children's sexual socialization during the middle school years information about sexuality needs to be provided.

1. Body safety such as rape and other forms of sexual abuse
2. Facts about AIDS, common sexually transmitted diseases, prevention, and treatment
3. Facts and dispelling of myths about pregnancy
4. Differences in sexual development
5. Differences regarding sexual orientation
6. Contraception
7. Masturbation

Table 7.1 Normal sexual development behaviors

Birth to preschool age	Elementary school age	Middle & high school age
Open, nonsecretive	Private self-exploration	Private self-exploration
Self-exploration	Masturbation	Masturbation
Masturbation		
Experimentation with different gender roles	Identification with a specific gender role	Specific gender role is established
Interest in seeing genitals of others during bathroom activities and play	May be repulsed or show increased interest in opposite gender sexual differences	Increased interest in sexual activities related to interactions between peers or adults
Sex play involves "playing doctor" or "house" including noncoercive sexual behaviors	Sexual behaviors include telling dirty jokes, kissing, hugging, holding hands	Petting, French kissing, mutual exploration of bodies, and (depending on socialization) digital penetration, oral, or anal sex, vaginal intercourse
Lack of inhibitions about personal nudity	Begins to seek privacy during dressing, bathing, and bathroom elimination	Exhibitionist behaviors such as mooning may develop

By providing information to parents, caretakers, and children (when approved by the legal guardian), children are more likely to have a less shameful and more informed sexual development. In addition, recognition of normal sexual developmental behaviors will provide a counselor with information to aid in assessing whether a child is displaying normal sexual developmental behaviors.

Article IV. Disruptions in Sexual Development

Disruptions, however, do occur in sexual development. Indirect exposure (finding pornography or observance of sexual activity) or direct exposure (sexual abuse) can result in confusion or the inability to process the information, and lead to acting out of the early experiences of sexual knowledge. Children may also react to oversexualized home environments, daycare experiences, or other adults or peer groups. Children through their sexual socialization are affected by observing activity in environments where sex takes place, and as a commodity (such as prostitution) or in exchange for food, shelter, or drugs. Whenever children's sexual knowledge exceeds their ability to process information related to sexual behaviors, and understand appropriate boundaries (usually between the ages of 3 and 7 years) there exists the possibility that these children will become sexually reactive. This refers to behaviors that include frequent masturbation, acting in a sexually provocative manner, and attempts to engage adults or other children in sexual behaviors that they have been exposed to. Sexually reactive children are not considered to be sexual offenders. Children who are sexual offenders will be referred to here as children who molest.

Article V. Sexually Reactive Children

Children may react to a variety of personal experiences or their environments and display sexualized behaviors. As a result of abuse or environmental factors, these children lack the lighthearted spontaneity and curiosity about sexual curiosity that exist in normal sexual development. These children experience shame, anxiety, and fear that result from disrupted sexual development. Sexualized children may have experienced or been exposed to:

- Sexual abuse
- Pornography
- Domestic violence
- Family nudity/sexual acts
- Physical abuse
- Recent stressful events

Domestic violence and physical abuse are often a part of sexually reactive children's home lives. An important developmental task for all children is learning to interact with others, establishing healthy emotional and physical boundaries, and engaging in socially appropriate behaviors. When children live in an environment where intrusive behaviors such as domestic violence or sexual abuse are occurring, they may not develop positive and nonintrusive social and sexual behavior. This can result in children who either do not recognize or are unwilling to respect other children's right to privacy and physical boundaries. These children are experiencing a combination of normal sexual curiosity and not having mastered healthy boundaries. These behaviors may be observed in child sexual play or reported by other children after exposure to another child who is sexually reactive.

Article VI. Assessing Sexual Behaviors between Children

When assessing whether sexual play between children is developmentally appropriate and normal, several factors should be considered.

- *Age of children:* An age difference greater than 2 years or greater in preschool and elementary school-aged children or 3 years difference in middle and high school-aged children, warrants further investigation. In addition, the intellectual age of the children should fall within their ranges.

- *Size:* Children develop physically at different rates. A disparity in size would become an important factor because of the possibility a smaller child may not be willing or may be afraid to establish boundaries within the limits of natural sexual curiosity.
- *Mutuality:* When the behaviors develop mutually and there is no evidence of coercion or manipulation, the incident may not be internalized as victimization.
- *Status:* Children who have been left in the care of a slightly older sibling experience a lack of equality or power that may result from being told to mind or listen to the older child. Another inequality exists when the other child is perceived to be more popular and has an elevated social status.
- *Type of sexual activity:* Sexual behaviors in children usually begin with self-exploratory behaviors then progress to genital curiosity about others during the first decade of life. Upon reaching puberty, children will normally begin to experiment with hand holding, kissing, which, depending on the sexual socialization of the children involved, will develop into mutual exploring of bodies, and then sexual activities such as intercourse or oral sex. Children who engage in escalated sexual behaviors such as 2- to 4-year-olds who perform oral sex on one another would be considered escalated.

When evaluating children's sexual play, any one of the above factors should alert the evaluator to the possibility of sexual abuse of one or more of the children involved. These behaviors should be reported to an appropriate child protective service agency (see chapter 8 for guidelines on reporting child sexual abuse).

In addition to sexual victimization, children who are exposed to excessive sexual stimulation through their environments experience sexual development disruption. Children experiencing stressful life events such as divorce, parental stress or violence, poverty, ethnic or racial discrimination, and school/peer difficulties may choose to deal with anxiety and their stressors through sexual activity. This can include excessive masturbation to calm and relax them or sexually acting out on others to gain power and control. Children who fall into the latter population may be progressing from sexually active to children who molest.

Article VII. Children Who Molest

The distinguishing difference between sexually reactive children and children who molest is coercion. Behaviors by children who molest may be associated with aggression, force, and manipulation. These children typically experience other difficulties such as anger management, academic failure, lack of social skills, and problem solving, and display minimal impulse control. Behaviors may be compulsive in that children will continue their activities despite requests to stop by other children or adults. Sexual interaction is not mutual between the children engaged in the sexual behaviors. Children who molest often threaten, bribe, and encourage secrecy in their victims. Children who molest sexualize most situations and their thoughts are dominated by sexuality. These children use sexual behaviors to cope with their emotions and the underlying motivation for action is not sexual. Behavior is directed this way to reduce emotional tension. Children who molest most often were victims of sexual abuse themselves, and they have not learned appropriate behaviors to cope with their own victimization. Counseling children who molest requires a focused set of components:

- Identification of emotional states — "Feeling Faces" in appendix
- Relaxation techniques — chapter 3
- Problem solving — chapter 5
- Social skills development — chapter 4
- Sexual behaviors boundaries — chapter 7 below

Article VIII. Educating Caregivers about Sexual Disruptions

It is imperative to provide education to parents and caregivers about masturbation, need fulfillment, and how to effectively respond to sexually reactive children and children who molest. Behaviors in these children may shock and disturb many parents or caregivers. It is helpful for these children's support systems to react calmly and not increase shame or emotional hurt that is the underlying motivation for many of these children's behaviors. Inappropriate reactions such as anger, spankings, or other punishment can actually increase sexual misbehaviors. Instead the focus will be on increasing effective ways children can meet their basic needs.

- *Survival:* Provide a nonabusive environment.
- *Love and belonging:* Believe, support, and demonstrate appropriate caring habits.
- *Power:* Encourage opportunities where children have control of events and activities that result in feeling safe and in control.
- *Freedom:* Allow choices and encourage creativity.
- *Fun:* Provide opportunities to participate in age-appropriate activities and discover new activities.

Parents and caregivers are responsible for establishing a safe environment that encourages limits, observes personal boundaries, and structures rules about how certain behaviors are displayed. This includes house rules focused on reducing sexual stimulation for children who are confused about sexual behaviors.

1. *Personal dress/nudity:* No walking around in underwear or sexualized clothing is permitted. Everyone is to keep clothing on when walking around the house. Knocking is required before entering rooms unannounced.
2. *Bedrooms:* No bed sharing or closed bedroom doors unless it involves one person.
3. *Play:* Children who are sexually reactive or molest will always be within visual contact with parents or caregivers. It is not necessary for caregivers to repeatedly verbalize this. It is the responsibility of caregivers to establish the rule, and then provide play environments that are appropriate. Playhouses, tents, and blanket play are discouraged. Wrestling, tickling, and other physical horseplay also has the possibility of being interpreted sexually.
4. *Affection/personal touch:* Initially, until it no longer appears appropriate, everyone within the house should ask permission before initiating personal touch such as hugging or kissing. Discourage others who attempt to elicit hugs or other touch after a child says "no." This applies to family members, teachers, other adults, and other children.
5. *Bathrooms:* Only one person in the bathroom at a time. Bathroom behaviors are to be private with the door shut. The only exception is with children under the age of 5 who require bathing and toilet assistance from an adult. Children, by the age of 3 can be taught that their penis, vagina, and rectum are private and provided with a washcloth to clean these areas.
6. *Sexual talk:* Healthy sexuality needs to be a part of the home environment. However, sexual jokes, innuendoes, music or television viewing that encourages sexuality through visual or auditory means should not be allowed.

Everyone in the household needs to follow the house rules, not just the children with the sexual misbehaviors. This reduces stigmatization, alienation, and promotes a healthy and safe atmosphere.

Intervening in children's sexual misbehavior may be uncomfortable for caregivers. It is important to separate children from their behaviors when responding. For example:

Table 7.2 Verbal responses to sexual acting out

Inappropriate response	Appropriate response
You are nasty.	That is against the rules.
That's bad.	Your behavior is inappropriate.
I am disgusted with you.	What you are doing is not OK.
What is wrong with you?	I want you to stop that behavior.

It is important to teach parents and caregivers how to react when they observe sexual misbehavior. It provides an opportunity for the caregiver to enforce house rules, teach new behaviors, and set limits without shaming or punishing. A technique that can be utilized to effectively confront sexual misbehavior involves stopping and identifying sexual misbehaviors, stating rules or expectations related to the behavior, encouraging a time for self-evaluation or redirection of behaviors.

1. *Stop the behavior:* Calmly separate the children or, in solitary activities such as private masturbation, ask the child to stop the behavior.
2. *Identify what behavior is inappropriate, and state expectations:* Clearly describe what the child is doing.
   "Bobby, it is not OK to touch Johnny's private parts."
   "Susie, it is against the rules to allow the dog to touch your private parts. Please put your pants back on."
   "Larry, it is not good to ask James to touch your penis."
3. *Encourage self-evaluation and redirection:* Depending on the age and cognitive development of the child, a brief time-out (see chapter 5) to reflect on the use of safe touches and personal boundaries can provide a child with a chance to think through the behaviors. Younger children may be better served by being casually redirected to another type of play or a different activity. Redirection can also provide the caregiver with an opportunity to organize their thoughts and response to sexual misbehaviors.

Article IX. Summary

Children's natural curiosity and abilities to experience the wonder of everyday life is upset by sexual abuse. Children can begin to neglect this need, which is critical to healing. Sexual abuse can also disrupt normal sexual development. Some children will become sexually reactive and in a worst-case scenario resort to molesting others to overcompensate for feelings of powerlessness, rage, and revenge. Every child who experiences sexual abuse will not become sexually reactive. In addition, sexually reactive children will not, with proper supervision, support, and education, become children who molest. Early intervention with families who are coping with sexual misbehaviors can provide reassurance that their children are not going to grow up to become adult sex offenders. Information about how to provide a healthy sexual environment, cope with sexual acting out, and the development of appropriate social interactions will lead children and their families in coping with a difficult and confusing set of behaviors. This process can be accomplished through a therapeutic environment that also encourages and incorporates fun.

CHAPTER 8

Reporting Abuse
Ethics and Cultural Competence

To see what is right and not do it is want of courage.

Confucius (551 B.C.)

Counselors, doctors, teachers, or any other helping professionals are not immune to poor decision making. Some of these circumstances will result from intentional decisions to ignore the ethical standards of their profession, and at other times will be due to a lack of awareness of laws or ethical guidelines. It is the responsibility of all professionals to educate themselves about specific ethical codes as they relate to areas within their scope of professional practice. Most professional organizations outline their ethical codes for behavior online.

When confronted with child sexual abuse in personal or professional environments, it is human nature to attempt to find explanations and ways to assimilate this information in order to personally cope with this horrific crime against innocence and to respond appropriately to children and their caretakers. In these situations, a professional can add to children's victimization by failing to provide adequate support, not reporting, minimizing and rationalizing, (see "Coping Behaviors," chapter 2), or not respecting appropriate therapist–client boundaries.

Article I. Responding to Disclosures

It is a difficult task to know how to respond appropriately to child sexual abuse. It requires both nonverbal and verbal actions to ensure that the response is perceived as warm, supportive, and safe. The following list suggests some of the guidelines that should be applied when working with children who are disclosing sexual abuse:

1. Physically move within arm's reach of the child and sit so that you are close to eye level.
2. Be aware of your nonverbal behaviors. Avoid crossed arms, leaning backwards or away from the child, and facial expressions that might be perceived as disgust, shock, embarrassment, or discomfort either with the disclosure or the child.
3. Encourage the child to talk freely and empower him or her to share only what the child wants to share. Disclosures often begin with small details in order for a child to gauge reactions to what he or she is telling and to determine trust.
4. Believe what you are being told. Circumstances such as parent–child conflicts or divorce often result in concerns about a sexual abuse disclosure. However, it is better to cope with believing a false report than neglecting a true disclosure.
5. Reinforce that disclosing was a good decision. Reflect the difficulty and courage involved in making the decision to tell about sexual abuse.
6. Reassure the child that he or she is not to blame. Let the child know that no matter what he or she did (accept money, gifts, or affection) or did not do (tell right away, yell, say stop), that sexual abuse is always the offender's fault.
7. Identify the child's current safety. Find out whether the alleged abuser is a threat to the child's safety, and whether a temporary housing plan (foster care or residential placement) is necessary to ensure safety until the alleged abuser can be found and dealt with by the legal system.
8. Determine a plan of action. Discuss and develop with the child and caregivers how the disclosure will be addressed. This typically includes a report to the county family and children social services or police department. A referral to a sexual assault physician may also be requested.

When making a report to social services or the police department, be prepared to provide the child's full name, birth date, and address. Also be ready to identify the name and whereabouts, if known, of the alleged offender. These details will allow a quicker response to the report. Write down as much information and details regarding statements and the child's emotional state during the disclosure. Do not rely on memory for details that may be requested at a later date. Educate yourself about reporting laws in the state in which you live. All 50 states in the United States of America have passed some form of a mandatory child abuse and neglect reporting law in order to qualify for funding under the Child Abuse Prevention and Treatment Act (1996). These laws require reporting by educators, law enforcement, mental health providers, licensed daycare providers, and physicians. Failing to report suspected abuse may result in criminal and civil liability as well as loss of professional licenses or other sanctions. It is not the responsibility of the professional reporting to prove that sexual abuse occurred. Anyone, including nonprofessionals, can report sexual abuse and be immune from prosecution as long as they report in "good faith."

Reporting sexual abuse often results in anxiety, confusion, and even fear for professionals. Remember that making a report does not mean that a professional accusation is being made. A report allows for more information to be gathered and assessed by appropriate service professionals. A determination can then be made as to how to proceed in a way that

Table 8.1 Rationalizations in reporting child sexual abuse

Rationalization for not reporting	Things to consider
1. The child will experience more problems/get in trouble at home.	Sexual abuse, if not stopped, has long-term emotional and physical effects. These may be reduced if the child is believed and receives psychological help.
2. The child lies a lot — he or she may not be telling the truth.	Sexually abused children often lie about many things because this has become a way to protect their abusers and hide the abuse in the past. Don't take a chance that the account of the abuse isn't true.
3. The child is from a "good family."	Families who look good also have stressors and they may need help learning to cope more effectively.
4. It's not that bad.	It's the law. Also the child may only be telling you a small part of what happened to see your reactions.
5. It happened a long time ago, "not recently."	The perpetrator is probably still active with other children.
6. It might not do any good. "I've reported before and nothing happened."	Not reporting means that the abuse will continue. It's important to help protect children.
7. If no abuse is determined, I'll be in trouble.	You only have to suspect sexual abuse to report. Making a report in "Good Faith" protects a person from legal prosecution.

addresses the safety and the legal and emotional needs of children and their families.

Personal issues, emotional responses, and biases can result in opportunities for a person to rationalize reasons not to report child sexual abuse. Many people hesitate and choose to not make the appropriate legal response.

Regardless of any justification or rationalization that can be developed, the most important factor to always remember is the safety and welfare of children. A person who makes a report is not responsible for proving sexual abuse occurred. This role belongs to the social service and legal systems. Children always need to be given the benefit of the doubt and all sexual abuse allegations should be reported. Each case will be investigated and steps taken to protect children. Even in situations where allegations are deemed unsubstantiated, children receive the benefit that one adult believed and attempted to help them.

In addition to making the appropriate decision to report suspected sexual abuse, mental health professionals are faced with many choices about how to deal with their therapist–client relationships. While there are many ethical considerations, the following areas will be addressed in this chapter: professional boundaries, confidentiality and values conflicts.

Article II. Professional Boundaries

When working with sexually abused children and their caregivers, it is important to recognize if the healthy boundaries of empathy, caring, and support begin to cross over to overresponsibility, overidentification, or intimacy conflicts. These behaviors by the therapist may include allowing clients to become involved in the therapist's personal life such as personal trips, outings, or visits to the therapist's home. Overinvolvement, romantic relationships, and ongoing socialization with the caregivers also constitute boundary violations.

Parenting of children in therapy by the professional is also unethical. Many children who enter counseling have been exposed to poverty, lack of affection/appropriate love and belonging, and other difficult circumstances. Therapists can sometimes violate the professional relationship by attempting to establish themselves as the loving parent children did not have. This type of relationship can further damage children's ability to recognize healthy relationships and boundaries. Therapists should self-evaluate their own motives and the long-term effects when they begin to demonstrate behaviors that may constitute this behavior.

- Buying gifts for nonclinical reasons.
- Cuddling or excessive touch.

- Throwing nongoal-oriented parties or celebrations.
- Allowing children to refer to the therapist as "parent," "aunt," "uncle," or other family references.

Article III. Sexual Misconduct by Therapists

Becoming romantically involved with older children or their caregivers is a definite boundary violation and is also sexually abusive because of the power differential involved between therapist and client. An inequality exists because children and their caregivers enter therapy in an emotionally vulnerable condition from doing their best to cope with sexual abuse in the family. Therapists who attempt to satisfy their own needs exploit the family and violate the trust that is crucial to the therapeutic relationship.

Therapists who are unaware of how to satisfy their own psychological needs in a healthy manner may be vulnerable to crossing boundaries. This occurs because counseling is an intense and intimate experience where people explore their deepest thoughts and feelings. When combined with a counselor who is not psychologically healthy, sexual abuse of the client can occur. Sexual abuse by a therapist can be covert or overt.

Section 3.01 Covert Sexual Abuse

Seductive behaviors include intense hugging, sexualized dress, sexual gazes, winks, smiles, or inappropriate facial expressions. Also included are flirting, secrets, and excessive attention to client or caretaker's dress and appearance.

Section 3.02 Overt Sexual Abuse

Sexual comments, kissing, sexualized jokes, fondling, or any form of sexual acts (intercourse, anal, oral, or digital penetration) are abusive.

The American Psychological Association (2003) also states that, not only are sexual relationships with current clients, their significant others, or relatives of the client unethical, but these boundaries also apply to a minimum of 2 years posttreatment. Even then, clients must be of legal age, have a stable mental condition, and not be viewed as possibly having any adverse effects from the relationship. Sexual attraction by therapists to clients has always occurred; however, little has been done to provide education or normalize this experience for mental health professionals. When left to cope with these issues alone, poor decisions can result that further sexually victimize clients. A national survey of sexual attraction by therapists to clients (Bernsen, Pope, & Tabachnick, 1994) was performed by sending out 1,000 surveys to clinical social workers. The results were as follows.

1. Most reported having had a sexual attraction to a client that resulted in guilt, anxiety, or confusion.
2. Some reported sexual fantasies about clients while engaged in sexual activities with someone other than the client.
3. A few (3.6% of men and .5% of women) reported actually having sex with a client.
4. Only 10% reported adequate graduate training about handling sexual attraction to clients.

In addition to lack of training in graduate programs, sexual misconduct by therapists may possibly be attributed to sexual behaviors modeled by graduate teachers and clinical supervisors who engaged in sexual relationships with their students. Pope, Levenson, and Schover (1979) revealed in their research that 10% of students engaged in sexual relationships with teachers/supervisors. These behaviors are inappropriate because of the status difference with teachers/supervisors who have more power by the fact that they can control grades and other academic outcomes. The impact of sexual relationships between students and teachers produced preliminary evidence to support the potential for future misconduct in their own professions after graduation. Their findings indicated that 23% of women who had sexual contact with educators reported later sexual contact with clients, as compared with 6% who did not have sexual contact with educators and had sexual contact as professionals with clients. This would suggest that graduate students who had been victimized by graduate teachers/supervisors need to address these issues through a therapeutic process to clarify appropriate boundaries for themselves and their clients in the future. The impact on clients who had been sexually involved with a therapist revealed a wide range of harmful effects (Pope & Vetter, 1991):

1. 90% of the patients were harmed by the sexual relationship.
2. 80% were harmed when the relationship began after termination of therapy.
3. 11% required hospitalization.
4. 14% attempted suicide.
5. 1% committed suicide.
6. 10% had experienced rape prior to the sexual relationship with the therapist.
7. One-third were victims of childhood sexual abuse or incest.
8. 5% were minors at the time of the sexual involvement with the therapist.
9. Only 17% of those reporting being harmed by the sexual relationship with a therapist indicated they had recovered fully from the experience.

A psychologically healthy therapist becomes aware of sexual or romantic attraction when it begins to occur and takes steps to address this issue instead of acting on it. Seeking supervision or consultation with a colleague is recommended in order to diminish feelings of isolation and uncertainty as to how to behave in the situation. It can be helpful to discuss the reasons for the attraction and whether a referral would be in the client's best interests.

When therapists are experiencing difficulty in their own personal relationships, they may need to consider seeking counseling in order to self-evaluate and explore behaviors to meet their need for love and belonging. It is necessary for therapists to not rely on clients or the families of clients to fulfill their basic needs.

Article IV. Multiple Relationships

Another area that ethical dilemmas often arise from is the issue of whether a situation constitutes a multiple relationship. Multiple relationships occur when the therapist is in a professional relationship with the client and at the same time involved in another role with a client (e.g., scout leader, purchasing a car, medical services) outside the therapeutic setting.

Therapists and clients often cross paths outside of the office setting, and in small towns it is impossible to imagine not having a multiple relationship on occasion. It is up to the therapist to carefully evaluate each situation and determine whether it is unethical and potentially harmful to the client's well-being. Some important self-evaluation questions should include:

1. Whose needs are being met by the additional relationship?
2. How long and how often will the contact occur outside of the professional relationship?
3. Is the client comfortable having contact with the therapist in this new environment?
4. If termination has occurred, is it possible the client will need to return for psychological services in the future?

Whenever the possibility exists that a multiple relationship could result in psychological stress for the client, steps should be taken to avoid the multiple relationship factors. If, for any reason, the relationship becomes long term, then a referral may be in the best interest of the client so that the boundaries of professionalism are not violated.

Article V. Confidentiality

In April 2003, the Health Insurance Portability and Accountability Act (HIPAA, 1996) went into effect. This law protects the privacy of all communications between patient and healthcare providers. Mental health providers must provide clients with information regarding their rights in written form, and prior to services. This includes how confidential information will be handled, protected, or released to other parties. Under most circumstances, the ability to release any information requires a written consent by a client. These releases generally include requests for information or permission to collaborate with current or previous (1) medical providers, (2) referral sources, (3) legal services, (4) insurance companies, (5) workers' compensation, and (6) additional parties to whom a client wants information provided. However, there are some circumstances a client should be made aware of in which information may need to be disclosed without consent.

1. *Clerical/financial/administrative staff:* Inform a client that these additional people who handle and manage their records are also bound by HIPAA standards. Some agencies that do not employ a full-time psychologist may also contract with professionals to sign off on records for insurance purposes. It is very important to inquire and document whether staff may call or send written documentation to a client's home.

2. *Case supervision/consultation:* It is often necessary to consult with other professionals or a clinical supervisor to discuss case management. These consultations should always be fully documented in the case record.

3. *Harm to self and/or others:* Mental health providers are obligated to act in order to protect the safety of a client or another in which harm has been indicated verbally or in written form. In circumstances where a client reports suicidal ideation or intentions, a counselor can contact family members of the client or seek hospitalization in order to protect the survival of the client. Additionally, if a therapist assesses that there is a probability of a client causing harm to another, he or she is obligated by a "duty to protect." This includes informing the potential victim and taking steps to reduce the possibility of harmful actions.

4. *Child/elderly abuse:* If abuse is known or suspected of a child under 18 years of age, to an elderly person, or to a physically or mentally disabled adult, a written report must be filed with a social service agency in the county where the abuse occurred. Written documentation on the case record should include to whom the report was made, when it was made, and what action the social service agency took.

5. *Court subpoenas/testimony:* Despite the fact that mental health records are covered as "privileged" by law, there are circumstances in which client records can be released. This includes when a court of law mandates the release by a court order. Client records may also be disclosed in the event of a lawsuit by a client against a therapist. Relevant information such as statements, assessments of functioning, and treatment interventions may need to be released in order for the mental health professional to protect his or her own liability.

6. *The child as the client:* Parents and caregivers should be made aware that to establish and maintain the trust necessary between therapist and child in order for therapy to be successful, they will be provided with limited information. This information includes attendance, general progress, treatment goals and plans, reported abuse, or imminent threats of harm to self or others.

By taking steps to become HIPAA compliant and disclosing any additional circumstances in which information can be shared, clients will understand that their professional records are private and their rights are respected. It is important to have clear documents outlining the professional standards of HIPAA compliance, with understandable explanations about the releases for disclosure of client information. When these standards are effectively in place the counseling relationship can move forward with a strong foundation where issues can be addressed without fear of recriminations.

Article VI. Cultural Diversity

During professional practice, therapists will encounter diversity in clients. Mental health care may be perceived differently by diverse groups; therefore therapists must be willing to adapt their treatment paradigms to adjust. Different cultures have varying norms on issues such as roles in the family, coping with adverse events, and stigma associated with addressing issues outside the family. Therefore it is critical to familiarize oneself as to the possible conflicts that may arise when working with different cultures. In addition, differences are a part of families within a culture. Therapists should always inquire about individual values, family values, and concerns about treatment in the initial assessment and throughout the therapeutic relationship.

These are some common areas in which values conflicts, bias, or limitations often occur in counseling and which require honest self-evaluation by therapists.

Gender	Sexual attitudes
Race/ethnic identification	Socioeconomic backgrounds
Sexual orientation	Physical/cognitive abilities
Age	Personal tastes (music, clothes)
Political views	
Language	
Religion	
Family values/roles	

Mental health professionals can benefit by asking themselves some of the following questions.

1. What are my opinions about people who have different values? Am I able to be professionally unbiased and provide help in an area that is not congruent with my ideas/values/beliefs?
2. As a professional, do I view it as my job to change the values or belief systems of others?
3. Do I have enough information about different cultures, sexual orientations, and persons with disabilities in order to provide an effective therapeutic environment?
4. Am I willing to admit my limitations and seek continued education and consultation in order to work with people's issues in areas in which I have limited knowledge?
5. How will I address the situation with the client referrals when needed?

An awareness of personal limitations or bias is important when accepting new clients for treatment. Counseling sexually abused children requires additional postgraduate training, supervised casework, and a high level of self-evaluation by therapists. Therapy with this population by counselors who do not understand sexual development in children, their coping reactions, and the effect of sexual abuse can cause additional emotional damage to children. On occasion, it is in the best interests of a client to provide a referral. Therapists should acknowledge that it is not necessary to be able to provide services to everyone, and not view professional decisions as personal weaknesses.

Article VII. Therapist and Survivor: Using Self-Disclosure with Clients

For therapists who are also survivors of childhood sexual abuse, this personal experience can be either advantageous or limiting. Therapists who have addressed the effects, taken stock, and learned to cope effectively can apply the strengths of the experience to their practice. Therapists should reference a personal life issue only after the difficulty has been resolved and not while it is an ongoing issue (Hunter & Struve, 1998). When gauged appropriately, therapists may choose to self-disclose in order to reduce a client's feelings of isolation and to offer support or real-life examples of emergence from victim to survivor. Self-disclosure is only appropriate when the goal of the disclosure is to meet the needs of clients. Self-disclosure, under appropriate circumstances, can add to the intimacy that is required in building a relationship with sexually abused children and with their caregivers. Some dangers, however, do exist when using self-disclosure as a tool in therapy:

1. The client may become overly focused on the therapist's issues or concerned how his or her own disclosure may cause harm through triggers and flashbacks.
2. The client may perceive the disclosure about how the therapist coped as a recommendation for his or her own behaviors.
3. The client may be overwhelmed and unable to express concerns due to the power differential.
4. In cases of excessive self-disclosure, inappropriate boundary violations may occur.
5. The therapist may continue to work through unresolved issues and focus on his or her own need fulfillment.

Therapists must be conscious of self-disclosure and attentive to how they impact the therapeutic relationship. Perhaps the most important determination in deciding when it is appropriate to self-disclose can be determined by two questions:

1. Is the purpose of this self-disclosure to meet the needs of the client?
2. Is the self-disclosure directly related to helping the client to meet a treatment goal or plan?

If the answer to both questions is "yes" then self-disclosure may actually benefit the therapy process. When a therapist is unable to give a definitive "yes," then it is preferable to avoid self-disclosure in the best interest of a client's well-being. Another important way to review whether self-disclosure will be useful is to discuss the use with colleagues or in clinical supervision.

Article VIII. Summary

Every therapist, at one time or other, will be faced with decisions about how to behave appropriately. The process of working through ethical dilemmas begins with (1) identification or awareness of a potential or real problem;

(2) seeking supervision or consultation; (3) knowing the ethical codes that are applicable to the situation; and (4) making a decision that is in the best interest of the client, therapeutic relationship, and personal/legal liability of the therapist. Through a heightened awareness of personal limitations, bias, and insight into their own psychological issues, therapists can prevent further victimization of their clients and families.

References

American Psychological Association, Council of Representatives. (2003). *APA ethics code*. Washington, D.C.

Anderson, C. A., & Bushman, B. J. (2002). The general aggression model: An integrated social-cognitive model of human aggression. *Annual Review of Psychology, 53*, 27-51.

Australian Institute of Health and Welfare. (2003). *Child protection Australia 2001-02*. Canberra: Australian Institute of Health and Welfare.

Badgley, R. (1984). *Report of the committee on the study of sexual offences against children and youths* (Vol. 1). Ottawa, Canada: Ministry of Supply and Services.

Bahr, A. (1988). *Sometimes it's ok to tell secrets*. New York: Putnam.

Bass, E. (1993). *I like you to make jokes with me, but I don't want you to touch me/me gusta que bromees conmigo, pero no quiero que me toques*. Lollipop Power. Chapel Hill, N.C.

Bass, E., & Davis, L. (1988). *The courage to heal: A guide for women survivors of child sexual abuse*. New York: Harper & Row.

Batsche, G. M., & H. M. Knoff. (1994). Bullies and their victims: Understanding a pervasive problem in the schools. *School Psychology Review, 23*(2), 165–174.

Baughman Jr., F. (2006). *The ADHD fraud: How psychiatry makes "patients" of normal children*. Victoria, BC, Canada: Trafford.

Becker, J., & Murphy, W. (1998). What we know and don't know about assessing and treating sex offenders. *Psychology, Public Policy and Law, 4*, 116–137.

Bernard, B. (1991). *Fostering resiliency in kids: Protective factors in the family, school and community*. Portland, OR: Northwest Regional Educational Laboratory.

Bernsen, A., Tabachnick, B., & Pope, K. (1994). National survey of social workers' sexual attraction to their clients: Results, implications, and comparison to psychologists. *Ethics and Behavior, 4*(4), 369–388.

Borg, M.G. (1999). The extent and nature of bullying among primary and secondary school children. *Educational Research, 41*, 137–153.

Bowlby, J. (1982). *Attachment and loss: vol. 1. Attachment*. New York: Basic Books. (Original work published 1969).

Breggin, P. R., & Breggin, G. R. (1995). The hazards of treating "attention-deficit/ hyperactivity disorder" with methylphenidate. *The Journal of College Student Psychotherapy, 10*(2), 55–72.

Briere, J., & Runtz, M.R. (1986). Suicidal thoughts and behaviors in former sexual abuse victims. *Canadian Journal of Behavioral Science, 18*, 413–423.

Child Abuse Prevention Treatment Act, 42 U.S.C.A. §5101 (West). January 1996.

Cockrum, J. R. (1999). *The study guide for choice theory, reality therapy and lead management.* Louisville, KY: Quality Development Seminars.

Crawford, D., Bodine, R., & Hoglund, R. (1993). *The school for quality learning.* Champaign, IL: Research Press.

Crittenden, P. M., & Ainsworth, M. (1989). Child maltreatment and attachment theory. In D.Cicchetti & V. K. Carlson (Eds.), *Clinical maltreatment: Theory and research on the causes and consequences of child abuse and neglect.* Cambridge, UK: Cambridge University Press, 432-463.

Crowder, A. (1995). *Opening the door: A treatment model for therapy with male survivors of sexual abuse.* New York: Brunner/Mazel.

Davis, S. (2005). *Schools where everyone belongs: Practical strategies for reducing bullying.* Champaign, IL: Research Press.

Dimock, P. T. (1988). Adult males sexually abused as children: Characteristics and implications for treatment. *Journal of Interpersonal Violence, 3*(2), 203–221.

Dunkelblau, E. (1999). January. Keynote address. American Association of Therapeutic Humor. Phoenix, AZ.

Erwin, J. (2004).*The classroom of choice: Giving students what they need and getting what you want.* Alexandria, VA: Association for Supervision and Curriculum Development.

Finkelhor, D. (1984). *Child sexual abuse: New theory and research.* New York: Free Press.

Finkelhor, D. (1994). Current information on the scope and nature of child sexual abuse. *The Future of Children, 4*(2), 31, 46–48.

Freeman, L. (1984). *It's my body/Mi cuerpo es mio.* Seattle, WA: Parenting Press.

Freeman, L., & Deach, C. (1985). *Loving touches.* Seattle, WA: Parenting Press.

Garland, R. J., & Dougher, M. J. (1990). The abused/abuser hypothesis of child sexual abuse: A critical review of theory and research. In J.Feierman (Ed.), *Pedophilia: Biosocial dimensions* (pp. 488–509). New York: Springer-Verlag,.

Gil, E., & Johnson, T. C. (1993). *Sexualized children: Assessment and treatment of sexualized children and children who molest.* Rockville, MD: Launch Press.

Gilgun, J., & Reiser, E. (1990). The development of sexual identity among men sexually abused as children. *Families in Society, 71*, 515–521.

Glasser, W. (1965). *Reality therapy.* New York: Harper & Row.

Glasser, W. (1975). *Schools without failure.* New York: Harper & Row.

Glasser, W. (1984). *Control theory.* New York: Harper & Row.

Glasser, W. (1989). *Reality therapy.* Harper & Row.

Glasser, W. (1992).*The quality school: Managing students without coercion.* New York: Harper Perennial.

Glasser, W. (1998a). *Choice theory in the classroom.* New York: HarperCollins.

Glasser, W. (1998b). *Choice theory.* New York: HarperCollins.

Glasser, W. (1998c).*The quality school teacher.* New York: Harper Paperbacks.

Glasser, W. (2000a). *Every student can succeed.* Black Forest Press.

Glasser, W. (2000b). *Reality therapy in action.* New York: Harper Collins.

Glasser, W. (2002). *Unhappy teenagers: A way for parents and teachers to reach them.* New York: HarperCollins.

Glasser, W. (2004*). Warning: Psychiatry can be hazardous to your mental health.* New York: HarperCollins.

Golden, G. S. (1991). Role of attention-deficit hyperactivity disorder in learning disabilities. *Seminars in Neurology ll* (1), 35–41.

Goldman, R., & Goldman, J. (1988). *Show me yours! Understanding children's sexuality.* New York: Viking /Penguin.

Gordon, S., Gordon, J., & Cohen, V. (1992). *A better safe than sorry book: A family guide for sexual assault prevention.* Amherst, NY: Prometheus Books.

Groth, N. (2001). *Men who rape: The psychology of the offender.* New York: Plenum Press.

Hartup, W. (1992). Having friends, making friends, and keeping friends: relationships as educational contexts. (ERIC Digest 345854).

Herman, J. L. (1997). *Trauma and recovery.* New York: Basic Books.

Hubbard, M. W., K. E. Glover, and C. P. Hartley. (2003). *HIPAA Policies and Procedures Desk Reference.* Chicago: American Medical Association.

Hoglund, R. (2006*). Educating for responsibility and quality: Intervention strategies.* Tempe, AZ: Bob Hoglund.

Holmes, W. C., & Slap, G. B. (1998). Sexual abuse of boys: Definition, prevalence, correlates, sequelae, and management. *Journal of the American Medical Association, 280*(21), 1855–1862.

Hunter, M. (1990). *Abused boys: The neglected victims of sexual abuse.* New York: Fawcett Columbine.

Hunter, M., & Struve, J. (1998). The ethical use of touch in psychotherapy. New York: Sage.

Johnson, T. C. (1992). *Let's talk about touching: A therapeutic game.* South Pasadena, CA.

Johnson, T. C., & Gil, E. (1992). *Sexualized children: Assessment and treatment of sexualized children and children who molest.* Self Esteem Shop II.

Julich, S. (2002). Breaking the Silence; Restorative Justice and Child Sexual Abuse. Ph.D thesis, Massey University, Auckland, NZ.

Katz, L. G., & McClellan, D. E. (1997). *Fostering children's social competence: The teacher's role* (ED 413 073). Washington, D.C.: National Association for the Education of Young Children.

Kawaljeet, K. (1999). Cultural prerequisites of freedom. *Indian Skeptic. 11(12).*

Krug, R. S. (1989). Adult male reports of childhood sexual abuse by mothers: Case descriptions, motivations and long-term consequences. *Child Abuse and Neglect, 13*(1), 111–120.

Lenett, R. (1985). *Kids have rights too!* New York: Playmore Publishers and Waldman Publishing.

Lisak, D. (1994). The psychological impact of sexual abuse: Content analysis of interviews with male survivors. *Journal of Traumatic Stress, 7*(4), 525–548.

MacMillan, H. L., Fleming, J. E., Trocme, N., Boyle, M. H., Wong, M., Rancine, Y.A., et al. (1997). Prevalence of child physical and sexual abuse in the community: Ontario health supplement. *Journal of the American Medical Association, 278*, 131–135.

Mathews, F. (1996). *The invisible boy: Revisioning the victimization of male children and teens.* Ottawa: National Clearinghouse on Family Violence, Health Canada.

Mathews, R., Matthews, J. K., & Speltz, K. (1989). *Female sexual offenders: An exploratory study*. Orwell, VT: The Safer Society Press.

Matsakis, A. (1991). *When the bough breaks*. Oakland, CA: New Harbinger.

Munro, Kali. (2000). *Male-to-male child sexual abuse in the context of homophobia*. Resources for Healing, http://www.KaliMunro.com.

National Commission of Inquiry into the Prevention of Child Abuse/England. (2005). *Statistics of education: Referrals, assessments and children and young people on child protection registers: Year ending 31 March 2004. London: NSPCC*.

Neumark-Sztainer, D., Story, M., Hannan, P., Beuhring, T., & Resnick, M. D. (2000). Disordered eating among adolescents: Associations with sexual/physical abuse and other familial/psychosocial factors. *International Journal of Eating Disorders, 28*(3), 249–258.

Olweus, D. (1993). *Bullying at school: What we know and what we can do*. Oxford, UK: Blackwell.

Pantley, E., & Sears, W. (2002). *The no-cry sleep solution: Gentle ways to help your baby sleep through the night*. New York: McGraw-Hill.

Pope, K., Levenson, H., & Schover, L. (1979). Sexual intimacy in psychology training: Results and implications of a national survey. *American Psychologist, 34*(8), 682–689.

Pope, K. S., & Vetter, V. A. (1991). Prior therapist–patient sexual involvement among patients seen by psychologists. *Psychotherapy, 28*(3), 429–438.

Roesler, T. A., & Wind, T. W. (1994). Telling the secret: Adult women describe their disclosures of incest. *Journal of Interpersonal Violence, 9*, 327–338.

Ryan, G. (1999). Treatment of sexually abusive youth: The evolving consensus. *Journal of Interpersonal Violence, 14* (4), 422–436.

Schwartz, D., Proctor, L. J., & Chien, D. H. (2001). The aggressive victim of bullying. In J. Juvonen & S. Graham (Eds.), *Peer harassment in school. The plight of the vulnerable and victimized*, pp. 147–174. New York: Guilford.

Sears, W., & Sears, M. (1995). *The discipline book: How to have a better-behaved child from birth to age ten*. Boston: Little, Brown.

Sears, W., & Sears, M. (2001). *The attachment parenting book: A commonsense guide to understanding and nurturing your baby*. Boston: Little, Brown.

Sears, W., & Sears, M. (2002). *The no-cry sleep solution: Gentle ways to help your baby sleep through the night*. New York: McGraw-Hill.

Sears, W., & Sears, M. (2003). *The baby book: Everything you need to know about your baby from birth to age two* (rev. ed.). Boston: Little, Brown.

Sedlak, A. J., & Broadhurst, D. D. (1996). *Third national incidence study of child abuse and neglect: Final report*. Washington, D.C.: U.S. Dept. of Health and Human Services.

Smallbone, S. W., & Wortley, R. (2001). Child sexual abuse: Offender characteristics and modus operandi. *Australian Institute of Criminology Trends and Issues in Crime and Criminal Justice, 193*, 1-6. Canberra: Australian Institute of Criminology.

Sullo, R. A. (1993). *Teach them to be happy*. Chapel Hill, NC: New View.

Sultanoff, S. (1992). The impact of humor in the counseling relationship. *Laugh It Up, Publication of the American Association for Therapeutic Humor*. July/August, 1.

Syed, F., & Williams, S. (1996). *Case studies of female sex offenders in the correctional service of Canada.* Ottawa: Ottawa Correctional Service, Canada.

Urquiza, A. J., & Goodlin-Jones, B. L. (1994). Child sexual abuse and adult revictimization with women of color. *Violence and Victims, 9*(3), 223–232.

U.S. Department of Health and Human Services. (2000). Child maltreatment. Washington, D.C.: Children's Bureau Crimes against Children Research Center.

van der Kolk, B. A., Perry, J. C., & Herman, J. L. (1991). Childhood origins of self-destructive behavior. *American Journal of Psychiatry, 148,* 1665–1671.

Vilaythong, A.P., Arnau, R.C., Rosen, D.H., & Mascaro, N. (2003). Humor and hope: Can humor increase hope? *HUMOR: International Journal of Humor Research, 16,* 79–89.

Wonderlich, S. A., Brewerton, T. D., Jocic, Z., Dansky, B. S., & Abbott, D. W. (1997). Relationship of childhood sexual abuse and eating disorders. *Journal of the American Academy of Child & Adolescent Psychiatry, 36*(8), 1107–1115.

Wubbolding, R. (1987). Professional ethics: Handling suicidal threats in the counseling session. *Journal of Reality Therapy, 7*(1), 12–15.

Wubbolding, R. (2000). *Reality therapy for the 21st century.* New York: Brunner-Routledge.

Appendix
Therapeutic Tools and Worksheets

Article I. Child Sexual Abuse Assessment Form

Child's Name: _____ DOB:_____ Gender: _____

Name of Person Filling out this Form: _____

Relationship to Child: _____

Referral Source: _____

Child's placement (home, foster care, youth home, detention): _____

_____

Name of Alleged Offender: _____

Current Location of Alleged Offender: _____

Will the Child be expected to Testify? _____ When? _____

Child's relationship to Offender:

Biological Parent_____

Adoptive Parent _____

Step-parent _____

Grandparent _____

Sibling_____Age of sibling _____

Other Relative_____Relation_____Age _____

Playmate _____Age _____

Babysitter _____Age _____

Stranger_____

Other_____Please explain _____

_____

Sexual Abuse Behaviors:

Fondling _____ Where?_____

Penetration: Anal _____Vaginal ____ Type: Hands _____Penis _____Object __

Oral contact to Child: Vaginal _____ Penis _____ Anal _____

Other_____

Oral Contact to Offender: Vaginal _____ Penis _____ Anal _____

Other_____

Exhibitionism _____Voyeurism_____Photography _____

Sexual devices_____Urination _____Defecation_____

Pornography _____Sexual talk _____Videotaping _____

Bondage _____Sex encouraged with other children ___

How long did the abuse occur?_____

Other behaviors or comments:_____

_____

_____

Other stressors:

Child's disclosure was not believed _____(explain) _____

_____

Residence changes (identify) _____

Parental divorce ____(when?) _____

School Changes ____(when?) _____

Out-of-home placement _____Identify _____

Financial changes _____Racism ____Homelessness _____

Physical abuse _____Domestic violence _____ Death _____

Previous sexual abuse _____

Academic/School problems _____Identify _____

Previous Mental Health History

Has the child been in counseling before? _____Dates _____

Name of Therapist _____

Reason for previous counseling _____

_____

Reason for ending treatment _____

_____

Has the child been evaluated by another psychologist/psychiatrist?_____

Name of evaluator_____

_____

Findings/Diagnosis_____

_____

Behavioral Concerns:

Suicide threats _____Spacing out _____Excessive lying _____

Anger _____Fire setting _____Shoplifting _____

Nightmares _____Separation anxiety _____Masturbation _____

Peer relationships ___Sadness _____Sleep problems _____

Perfectionism _____Sexual orientation _____Pulling hair out _____

Drugs/Alcohol _____(explain) _____

Self-injury _____(explain) _____

Suicide attempts ____Date(s) _____

Fears _____(identify) _____

Eating problems (identify) _____

_____

_____

Medical problems (identify) _____

_____

_____

Sexual acting out (explain) _____

_____

_____

_____

Other concerns not listed _____

_____

_____

_____

Treatment Expectations

What do you think are the child's most immediate treatment concerns? ____

_____

_____

Other professionals involved in case: (Social Services, Detectives, CASA, Prosecutor, Attorneys, etc.) _____

_____

_____

	Name	Phone #	Role
1.			
2.			
3.			
4.			
5.			
6.			

Fig. A.1 Feeling faces chart.

Something I feel excited about	Something I feel scared about
Something I feel mad about	Something I feel worried about

Fig. A.2 Feelings worksheet.

Feeling Worksheet 2

When I feel _____

It is _OK_ for me to:

It is <u>NOT OK</u> for me to:

Fig. A.3 Feeling worksheet 2.

What Do I Want?

1. What do I want?

_____

_____

2. What am I doing that prevents me from getting what I want?

_____

_____

3. What am I willing to do that is different?

_____

_____

4. What needs am I trying to meet by my current behaviors?

_____

_____

5. What can I do differently to meet my needs?

_____

_____

_____

Perceived Value Adjectives

afraid	disappointed	imaginative	rich
alert	discouraged	impolite	rowdy
angry	dishonest	inconsiderate	rude
annoyed	disrespectful	independent	sad
anxious	doubtful	innocent	safe
apologetic	down	intelligent	scared
attentive	eager	jealous	secretive
average	easygoing	kind	selfish
bad	embarrassed	lazy	serious
bored	encouraging	leader	shy
bossy	energetic	lively	silly
brave	evil	lonely	sly
bright	excited	loving	smart
busy	fair	loyal	sneaky
calm	faithful	lucky	sorry
careful	fearless	mature	spoiled
careless	foolish	mean	stingy
cautious	fortunate	messy	strange
charming	friendly	miserable	stubborn
cheerful	frustrated	mysterious	sweet
childish	funny	naughty	talented
clever	gentle	nervous	thankful
clumsy	giving	nice	thoughtful
concerned	glamorous	noisy	thoughtless
confident	gloomy	obedient	tired
confused	good	obnoxious	tolerant
considerate	grateful	old	touchy
cooperative	greedy	peaceful	trusting
courageous	grouchy	picky	trustworthy
cowardly	guilty	polite	unfriendly
cruel	happy	poor	unhappy
curious	hateful	popular	upset
dangerous	healthy	positive	useful
daring	helpful	proud	weak
dark	honest	quiet	wicked
demanding	hopeful	rejected	wise
dependable	hopeless	reliable	worried
depressed	humorous	responsible	
determined	ignorant	restless	

False Beliefs

- The abuse was my fault.

- I am helpless.

People will not like me if they know.

People will think I am gay if they know.

- My body is disgusting/betrayed me.

I must be perfect to overcome this.

- No one else has had this happen.

I deserved this.

What I want doesn't matter.

I must protect my family at all cost.

My feelings are bad/stupid/don't matter.

Trusting people is dangerous.

If I am unattractive I won't be abused again.

I am dirty/broken/used.

I feel guilty.

Sex is bad/confusing/a way to get my needs met.

Fig. A.4 False beliefs created by sexual abuse.

Picture Me!

HOW I SEE MYSELF

HOW OTHERS SEE ME

HOW I WANT TO BE SEEN

HOW I WANT OTHERS TO SEE ME

Fig. A.5 Picture me.

Things I Feel Proud About

_____

1. _____

2 _____

3. _____

4. _____

Fig. A.6 Things I feel proud about.

Things I Do Well

Fig. A.7 Things I do well.

How I Have Fun

Fig. A.8 How I have fun.

What I Feel Happy About

Fig. A.9 What I feel happy about.

Things I Would Like to Learn

Fig. A.10 Things I would like to learn.

Fig. A.11 My favorite memory.

Fig. A.12 Something I overcame.

1. _____

2. _____

3. _____

Fig. A.13 Three wishes.

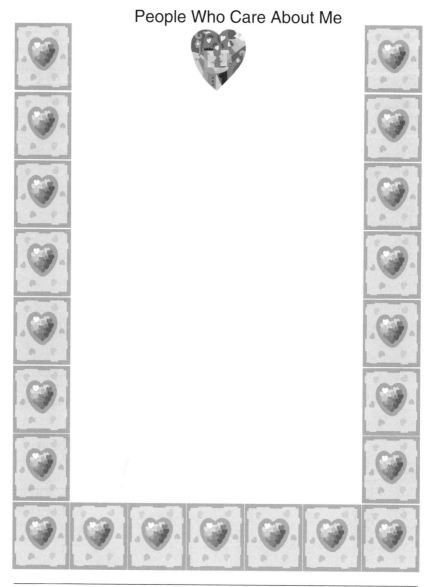

Fig. A.14 People who care about me.

Table A.4 Helping or hurting?

Choices I am making now.	Is this hurting or helping me?	Choices I would prefer to make.	How will this help me?

Table A.5 Meeting my needs

Survival	Love & belonging	Power	Freedom	Fun

Fig. A.15 Don't put all your eggs in one basket.

Something I Get Angry About

What I Do When Angry

Fig. A.16 Something I get angry about.

Article II. Think-About-It Form[*]

Date: _____

Name: _____

1. What did you do?
   Please be specific. Start with "I." Tell me later about what the other student did.

   _____

   _____

2. Why was that the wrong thing to do?
   Who did you hurt? How do you know you hurt them?

   _____

   _____

3. What problem were you trying to solve?
   Did you want attention? Did you want to be left alone? Were you trying to have fun?
   Were you already mad about something else?

   _____

   _____

4. Next time you have that problem, how will you solve it without hurting anyone? *Please list three ways to solve the problem.*

   _____

   _____

   _____

[*] This worksheet is from *Schools Where Everyone Belongs* by Stan Davis, Research Press, 2005, and is used with permission. More ways to use it effectively can be found in that book.

 _____

_____

_____

_____

_____

_____

Fig. A.17 Choices I made today.

Index